— THE —
ONLY CHILD

Friends of the Oregon City
Public Library
USED BOOK STORE

THE ONLY CHILD

*Being One, Loving One,
Understanding One, Raising One*

Darrell Sifford

PERENNIAL LIBRARY

Harper & Row, Publishers, New York
Grand Rapids, Philadelphia, St. Louis, San Francisco
London, Singapore, Sydney, Tokyo, Toronto

Selections from *When All You've Ever Wanted Isn't Enough* by Harold S. Kushner, copyright © 1986 by Kushner Enterprises, Inc. Reprinted by permission of Summit Books, a division of Simon & Schuster, Inc.

From the book *The Birth Order Book* by Kevin Leman, copyright © 1985 by Dr. Kevin Leman. Used by permission of Fleming H. Revell Company.

Selections from *Forgive & Forget* by Lewis B. Smedes, copyright © 1984 by Lewis B. Smedes. Reprinted by permission of Harper & Row.

This book was originally published in hardcover in 1989 by G. P. Putnam's Sons It is reprinted by arrangement with G. P. Putnam's Sons, a division of The Putnam Publishing Group.

THE ONLY CHILD. Copyright © 1989 by Darrell Sifford. All rights reserved. Printed in the United States of America. No part of this book may be used or reproduced in any manner whatsoever without written permission except in the case of brief quotations embodied in critical articles and reviews. For information address Harper & Row, Publishers, Inc., 10 East 53rd Street, New York, N.Y. 10022.

First PERENNIAL LIBRARY edition published 1990.

LIBRARY OF CONGRESS CATALOG CARD NUMBER 89-45717

ISBN 0-06-097288-2

90 91 92 93 94   FG   10 9 8 7 6 5 4 3 2 1

Acknowledgments

This book truly is the result of a team effort, and I want to thank the many people, friends and strangers alike, who shared themselves, their opinions and their stories, who canceled appointments when it was necessary to make time for me, who supported my work and let me know in so many ways how important they thought it was.

I especially appreciate the help of my agent, Jane Dystel, who always said the right thing at the right time; my editor, Judy Linden, who championed this book and who was a delight to work with; my only-child friend Maurice Prout of Hahnemann University, who made available to me the doctoral dissertation of Micah Altman, *The Gender Role Development of the Only Child,* which reviewed much of the formal research on only children.

To my father and my mother,
whose love at times surpassed my understanding

Contents

Prologue

At ten minutes past four o'clock on the afternoon of Saturday, September 19, 1931, I entered the world and, as would become customary, there were just the three of us: my mother, my father and me. The doctor didn't get to our house until a few minutes later.

As an only child, I grew up emotionally and physically close to my parents. When they went somewhere, I went along. Part of that was dictated by economics. My father was wiped out in the Great Depression, and there was no money for babysitters. But beyond that my parents conveyed to me the sense that we were a three-some, that we belonged together until any one of us felt the need for more space. I never felt that need until I was an adolescent, and then I was given all the space I could handle. I grew up thinking that the world really was my oyster. I felt secure, loved, valued, important, comfortable in the limelight, very much at the center of my own little universe. My parents always had time for me, whenever I asked, but they always waited for me to ask. I can't remember a single time when my father, no matter how busy or tired he was, declined to play ball with me. He never even suggested that we wait a few minutes. I can't remember a single instance when my mother, even after she went back to work, told me that, no, it wasn't possible for her to grill me a hamburger or prepare her wonderful chili that would have driven the competition in South Texas out of business if she'd ever gone commercial with it.

Was I spoiled—an unbridled brat? This is, after all, a charge that so often is leveled against the only child. I never thought of myself as spoiled, but, yes, in some ways I suppose I was. Growing up, I did get some bloody noses, symbolically and even literally, until I learned that the world wasn't always going to drop everything and play ball with me or serve up my favorite meal whenever I wanted. But the best thing I got from growing up as an only child with remarkable parents was an image of self-worth that was both realistic and enduring. I like myself and, because I do, I'm able to like other people, too; to respect them, work with them, share with them, rejoice in their triumphs, feel the sting of their defeats.

Not all only children, of course, are so fortunate, but many are, and in this book you will meet some of them, those who have climbed their highest mountains, not because they were driven to do it, but because they chose to do so. You also will meet only children who have struggled mightily because of unfortunate parenting, as well as therapists who have worked extensively with only children, their parents, spouses, friends and, in some cases, their foes.

This is a book that I have known I would write for many years, a book to strip away the stereotypes and examine objectively the only child. For years, even before I began serious work on the book, I routinely piggybacked questions about only children onto other interviews for my newspaper column. "Are you an only child? Hey, tell me about it."

This book will picture the only child in a light that has been seen too seldom, as a person with unique strengths who is able to overcome the disadvantages and build on the assets inherent in growing up in the spotlight. In sharing some of my own experiences and those of others, I realize that some only children may not identify with all of them. But I think that they can learn from these experiences because the many interviews present a broad picture of what it means to be an only child, to be the parent of an only child, to be married to an only child. This is a book that will leave only children feeling good about themselves, in a realistic sort of way, and hopefully it will help guide them to change the parts of themselves that they and others don't like.

This is a book about people, their lives, told sometimes in their own words, and it is by nature mostly anecdotal. It is not a book based on what researchers would call hard data, the kind you can take into a laboratory, dissect and hold up to the cold light of scientific scrutiny. A primary reason for this is that, surprisingly, there has been very little scientific research into the only child. The research that has been done over the years tends for the most part to be inconclusive and contradictory. Researchers who seem to be trying to find answers to similar questions often emerge with radically different results. Part of this may be because the samples of only children who have been studied are relatively small. Part of it may be because the researchers used different methods and tried to mix apples and oranges. Part of it may be because those who study the only child, like those who study a lot of other things, tend to find what they're looking for, by dismissing as insignificant anything that falls outside their desired pattern.

So what we're left with are the stereotypes, most of which are negative and, unfortunately, widely believed: The only child is selfish, handicapped, anxious, not fun to be with, egotistical, at a disadvantage when it comes to making his own way in a world that doesn't automatically thrust him onto center stage. In years past, more than a few therapists, in their writing and lecturing, have loaded some heavy burdens on the only child: The only child has difficulties with every independent activity and sooner or later becomes useless in life. . . . Being an only child is a disease in itself. . . . The only child lacks independence, self-confidence and practical skills. . . . The only child is depressed and cautious, and needs to be the center of attention.

Most of these views were advanced long ago, but the stereotypes continue to this day. Hahnemann University psychologist Maurice Prout, himself an only child, explains how this happens: "Case studies have fostered a series of myths about only children, and mostly that's what we're dealing with—myths. You hear a therapist lecture about the only child, and you accept those myths. Then you go back to your office and your first client is an only child who's depressed or anxious, and it fits all the negatives you've just heard in the lecture, and you say 'Yes, he's that way because he's an only child. What else could you expect?' But what nobody thinks about is that the guy down the street is depressed or anxious, too, and he's the third of five children, but nobody says he's that way because he's the third child."

I've even found myself buying into the stereotypes at times. I would have bet my boots that Donald Trump, the real-estate developer with the Midas touch, was an only child. After all, he has incredible ambition and drive, and he won't accept defeat or take no for an answer. I was certain he's this way *because* he is an only child. What a great interview he would provide for this book, I thought. But, surprise: Donald Trump is the fourth of five children. Do you suppose that's why he's the way he is?

Yes, it can get confusing and out of hand, exploring a subject that is so long on myth and so short on actual research. One psychiatrist I interviewed for this book told me not entirely in jest that the only child was a magnificent area for me because "whatever you write, nobody can prove it's not true." Be that as it may, here are some things that I feel comfortable saying about the only child, parents and the family:

· Somewhat more than twenty percent of married couples in the United States have one child, and it's generally agreed that the trend is growing. This is being caused mainly by two factors, the first of which is the economy: It's so expensive these days to bring up and educate children that many couples are deciding that, realistically, one child is all they can afford. This applies to couples who adopt a child, too, since the cost of adoption through a private agency can run as high as $25,000. The second factor is that more couples, determined to establish their careers, are waiting until later, almost on the edge of midlife, to have their first child. They're reluctant, because of age, to have any more. In addition, because they're older, they understand more clearly the difficulties of parenting and, in the words of one child-development expert, "some feel that one is about all they can handle."

· How the only child is parented is determined to a considerable extent by whether he is an only child by choice or by fate, biological or otherwise. Parents who would like to have several children but who can have only one seem prone to load some of their disappointment on the only child and to create in that child special problems that, unless dealt with professionally, can last a lifetime. A classic message that disappointed parents pass on to the only child is this: "You're all we've got, and, by God, you'd better be everything to us all of the time." It's an impossible prescription to fill, of course, and everybody suffers, most of all the only child, who feels like a failure. On the other hand, parents who have an only child by choice tend to be more relaxed and more realistic in their expectations. Demographically, these parents tend to be better educated than the population in general, more liberal, older, more successful in their careers, less influenced by what others think—all of which are positive factors in parenting.

· The only child is more often male than female (although in the general population it is females who outnumber males). This is based not on any actual count but on the intuitive feeling of many therapists that couples, mother and father alike, have a deep yearning for a son who will carry on the family name. If the first child is a girl, they may try again. But if the first child is a boy, they may stop there. A psychiatrist told me "whenever I think of an only child, I always think of a male. Why? I don't know, except that in my whole lifetime I've never had as a patient one woman who was an only child. But I've had lots of men."

· The only child is more androgynous than children with siblings and is more prone to cross-play with boy-girl toys. There is less sexual-role stereotyping, and one reason seems to be that there's no sibling around to chastise the only child: "Don't you know that boys don't play with dolls?" That androgynous adults are happier and better adjusted than adults who cling doggedly to sexual-role stereotyping seems beyond serious challenge.

· Some of the problems that only children encounter may stem not from being only children but from being from a divorced home and brought up by one parent. Mothers of only children have a divorce rate that is twice as high as mothers of two to four children, and this is one reason for their having an only child.

· Mental health studies indicate what is described as an "insignificant tendency" for only children to be overrepresented among those with maladjustment and neurosis and underrepresented among those with behavior problems and sociopathology. In other words, only children are pretty much like everybody else, and a great deal of what applies to only children also applies to children with siblings, not only in the area of mental health but in many other areas, too.

· The only child ranks second in intelligence, as measured by tests, to the first-born child with one or two siblings even though the only child typically gets more individual attention from parents. This seeming advantage is offset, apparently, by the impact of mentoring siblings and learning from siblings. However, the only child is more highly motivated, attains higher levels of formal education, has more lofty career ambitions. Nobody is quite sure why this is the case, but a reasonable explanation is that the only child is primed more by parents to reach for the stars. If you believe the people who make their living by looking into such matters, you find that the only child is disproportionately represented among high achievers—astronauts, star athletes, Pulitzer Prize–winners, scientists, eminent composers, actors and actresses. Somebody even determined that only children are pictured disproportionately on the cover of *Time* magazine. Among the world's best-known only children are Charles Lindbergh, Albert Einstein, Indira Gandhi and Franklin D. Roosevelt.

· The only child spends a lot of time alone, and the result of this can run the spectrum from being shy and lonesome to being confident and self-starting. At its best, being an only child can enhance the ability to work independently, to use your own initiative, to draw your own conclusions and solve your own problems. These are qualities prized in the professions and in business.

· Because he tends to be perfectionistic to meet parental expectations, the only child is less tolerant of his own mistakes, less casual about imperfections and struggles more than other children with the gap between his ideal self-image and his actual self-image. A major task for parents of an only child is to help the child learn to accept limitations and develop a realistic self-image.

· The only child often feels that he has grown up before his time. Part of the reason for this is that parents frequently teach the only child adult skills. The only child often appears to be a little adult, more confident around grown-ups than peers. Some only children have complained to me that they felt as if they never had a childhood. A challenge for parents: Always remember that the only child is still a child, and treat him that way—with love and respect, but as a child.

· The only child has a strong need to feel special, a need based on his recognition that he's the star player in the family game. There's nobody to dilute attention and praise, nobody to whom he is compared. Once this pattern is set early in life, he struggles if he doesn't get "enough" from parents and other significant people, such as teachers. In the words of an only-child psychiatrist, "Parents had better be able to make him feel special—at least at times. If the only child doesn't find a lot of specialness in the relationship, he will be unhappy." What can parents do to make the only child feel special? That's up to individual parents to decide, but the important thing is that they understand this is an important need of the only child.

· The only child who complains bitterly about not having siblings, who talks often about feeling cheated or shortchanged, tends not to speak positively about the relationship with the parents. This suggests to me that these only children in reality may be criticizing their parents but, because they aren't comfortable doing this head on, focus their criticism on lack of siblings instead. It is rare for me to meet an only child who speaks lovingly of his relationship with his parents and who simultaneously expresses resentment over not having brothers or sisters. I think it may come down to this: All parents load a lot of stuff on their children, but especially on the only child. If most of it is good stuff, the child isn't eager to share it with anybody else. But if most of it is bad, the child, quite understandably, would like to have siblings who could shoulder some of the burden.

I've covered a lot of ground in this book, and what I emphasized, downplayed or left out altogether was based solely on my subjective judgment. The more I study the only child, the more I realize how much remains to be written, by me or somebody else.

In gathering my stories, I interviewed hundreds of people, some of whom allowed their names to be used. You'll be able to recognize them because they are identified by their real names. Other people didn't want their real names used, so I created names for them. Many of the people I interviewed face-to-face; some were interviewed by telephone, others by mail. In a few instances I never met the people at all, and their stories were told to me by therapists relying on case histories. But all of the people are real, and there are no composites presented as one person.

I've had a good time working on this book, and in some ways it's been therapeutic for me—helping me understand better why I am the way I am and giving me insights into how I might alter some of what still rises up occasionally and bites me, even after all these years. I hope you have a good time reading this book and find it helpful.

DARRELL SIFFORD
Philadelphia
March 1988

──── 1 ────

Lonely Only or Secure Soloist?

It was Jefferson City, Missouri, four o'clock in the morning. Lights were on in only one house on the block-long street that clung to the hillside, a sturdy red-brick house with white trim and a full porch, the classic architecture of the 1920s.

Inside the man and his wife shuffled from room to room for what they knew would be the last time. They stood in the bedroom in which his parents had slept and loved for so many years.

"It looks so empty . . . and so forlorn," the man said.

The woman held his hand but said nothing. She pushed shut the closet door to block the sight of dresses, blouses, skirts and coats that hung neatly, clothing that hadn't been claimed by friends, clothing that mutely awaited the auctioneer who would appear in a few days and offer it to the highest bidder, along with everything else that remained.

The man and his wife mounted the stairs to the attic for a final look at what they painfully had decided to leave behind because there was no way to take it all back to their home in Philadelphia: the games that the man, as a little boy, had played with, the baseballs, the bats, the sports magazines from the 1940s, the colorful aluminum tumblers from which icy lemonade had been gulped by the tiny grandsons so many times.

"We've got to go now," the man whispered. "It'll take us three hours to get to St. Louis and check the car in at the airport."

"I know," the woman said.

Room by room they clicked off the lights and when they reached the front door, the man did a strange thing. He spoke to the house. "Goodbye. I hope the next people are good to you. You deserve it."

Then he sealed the keys in an envelope, which he slipped into the mailbox for the real-estate broker to retrieve later in the day.

In heavy silence they backed the rental car out of the driveway and lingered for a moment in the street.

"I never knew anything could hurt this much," the man sobbed. "Oh, God, I wish I'd come home last week. I wish I'd been here."

The woman cried, too. She kissed the man and said: "I loved your mother, too."

They drove down the hill, and neither looked back.

As a boy, I was closer emotionally to my father than to my mother, yet when he died in 1978 my grief, although it was choking, did not equal what I suffered when my mother died six years later.

Why? I've asked myself that many times, and now finally, with the grieving behind me, I believe that I have an answer.

When Dad died, I turned much of my concern toward Mom, who had been his companion for fifty-four years. Could she survive such a blow? Would she even want to survive? What could I do to help her?

When Dad died, I still had a parent and a family home, a place to come to at special times. I still had somebody to whom I could write special letters, mail my newspaper columns and send funny cards on birthdays and holidays. I still had somebody to whom I was a child and from whom radiated the kind of no-strings love, acceptance and understanding that only a parent truly can offer.

When Mom died, all of that died, too. The connection to childhood was severed, except in memories, and, as an only child, I felt so terribly alone. For the first time in my life I wished for brothers and sisters.

It's an Old Song, So Familiar

An only child.

So terribly alone.

Yes, that's what we've all been told, and couples wondering if they should have more than one child so often hear: "It would be a mistake to have just one. Why, he'd be all by himself . . . and he'd get spoiled rotten."

The only child has been called "the lonely only." He's also widely regarded as perfectionistic, self-centered, rigid, so tuned in to achievement that he tramples on everybody and everything to get the gold star and move to the head of the class. They say that the only child can't forgive and forget, can't deal with disappointment and failure, is closed-minded, has feelings of infallibility and really believes at the core of his soul that, if push came to shove, he could walk on water without getting his shoes damp.

Like every other person who is stereotyped, the only child can't just say it's all rubbish. This is because there is enough truth in these generalizations to warrant his attention. But basically I think that the only child has been the victim of a lot of bad press. There are pluses that nobody talks about much and, if the only child talked about them, wouldn't he be seen as tooting his own horn? Not infrequently the only child speaks with action rather than words. This is at the root of much achievement—the desire to shatter the stereotype.

I've been interested in the life of the only child ever since I was old enough to understand that I was one, that I was in some ways different from the other kids.

They interacted comfortably with each other, while it was a chore for me. They understood how group games were played; I hung back and tried to learn. They couldn't wait to grow up and get away from their parents; I liked being at home with two people who treated me with love and consideration. They needed action or else they complained that they didn't have anything to do; I picked up a book, wrote a short story, dreamed a fantasy. They thrived on noise; I savored peace and quiet.

Because I, as a writer, have pursued my interest in the only child, I have a definite perspective on what it means to be one. The bottom line, as I see it, comes to this: Yes, I and many only children really *are* different from those with siblings in some fundamental ways, but the ways in which we are different are not necessarily negative—to us or anybody else. We do have our quirks and we can't deny or hide them for very long. But we also have many good things going for us, things that tend to get overlooked in society's seeming rush to point out what's wrong with only children. We tend to be highly motivated, hard-working, comfortable with solitude, punctual, creative.

Many of us are confident in the spotlight, and if you talked with enough outstanding public speakers, you'd find that many of them are only children. Why? Because we're so accustomed to getting attention, it's not difficult for us to attract the attention of others. When we get on the podium, we feel that everybody should listen to us . . . and they do. A while back I read a self-help book that encouraged people, no matter how shaky they felt, to act as if they were better than everybody else. The payoff, the book promised, was that if you act that way people will assume you *are* better and treat you that way. You know what? It's really true, and when it can be done in a nonmalicious sort of way, it helps you and doesn't hurt anybody. Only children, I am convinced, have understood this from the first day, and many of us have used it to our advantage in our professional lives. If there's one thing that only children, as a group, tend not to lack, it's self-confidence. In some ways we're like the two-million-dollar shortstop who, when the bases are loaded, wants the ball hit at him because he knows that he can handle it.

If we're lucky, we have been well loved by our parents in a wholehearted way that was not diluted because our parents had to share it, and their energy, with other children. If we're lucky, we have known that we are special, and we have the foundation to love others because we love ourselves.

That's the Word, Love

Psychiatrist Leon Saul, a leader in the development of psychoanalytical training in the United States, once told me that parenting, in its purest form, came down to one simple thing: love.

If parents truly love the child and if they show it in a way that the child perceives it, they need not worry about how their child will turn out. "Parents can make a lot of mistakes, even some bad mistakes," said Saul, but the child will be resilient enough to bounce back without damage because the child feels loved, accepted, valued. On the other hand, a child who does not feel loved may not have the strength to survive the mistakes of parenting.

An analogy: The person who has grown up with money, who is accustomed to having money, always feels that he is wealthy, even when he is virtually penniless. His feeling is: "I'm a wealthy person who at the moment happens to be without funds." Conversely, the person who has grown up without money always feels poor, even if the bank account is bulging: "I'm a poor person who at the moment happens to have some wealth."

So it is with love . . . or without love. "I am a person who is loved, a worthwhile person who at the moment is encountering some static." Or: "I'm not lovable, and the good things that are happening to me at the moment soon will pass, and I'll be miserable again."

What I got as an only child from parents who let me know they loved me without qualification was the sense that I could try to do anything I wanted to do and, if it didn't work out, I could try something else. Whatever happened, I was okay. Mom and Dad had told me that, and they had shown me, too.

Only children, if they're lucky, do feel special. Cyndi, an only child, was given a rather common name with a decidedly uncommon spelling. For years she didn't think much about it, but then it occurred to her that her parents must have had a reason for it. When she asked, she was told by her mother: "You are so special to us, and we wanted you and the world to know that you're not just another Cindy."

If they don't have decent relationships with their parents, only children often blame themselves and see themselves as lacking what it takes to make it in the world. The way in which the only child develops is shaped by the same factor that influences all children—that factor is the parents, and it can be said boldly that the effects of parenting are magnified on the only child because there are no other children around to dilute those effects. The only child gets it all, the good and the bad, and more than anybody else in the world, the only child is the product of parenting.

Understanding a Father's Wounds

My father, who was in all ways the model of a kind, loving man, spoiled me in the sense that he probably said yes too often and no not often enough. Maybe because I was an only child he spoiled me even more, but the way he treated me was a direct result of the wounds that he suffered in childhood.

He was the son of a small, arrogant man with a large, bushy mustache, a man of violent temper and foul language, a man who built himself up by tearing others down. Most of all he tried to tear down the boy who would become my father. I saw pictures of him, but I never met him; he died long before I was born. I think I would have hated him. I think perhaps my father hated him, after he got old enough to understand that hate, like love, had to be earned and that his father had worked hard for it and had earned it.

There were four sons and one daughter, and clearly the favored child was the first-born, Alec, who was a couple of years older than my father. They lived on a farm in Arkansas, and they worked the way farmers work: all day. One afternoon the boys quit early, because of a severe rainstorm, and later, when the clouds cleared away, they went swimming in a muddy, angry creek.

Alec went in headfirst, and he didn't come up. It was hours before they found his body. In silence they grieved, and nobody talked about the agony that everybody felt. Then one day the arrogant man with the mustache spoke.

He and my father were setting fence posts, just the two of them. He looked down at Dad, who was positioning a post in a hole, and said: "I wish it had been you instead of Alec."

Dad told me that story after I was grown, and he cried and I cried, and we hugged each other, as a way, almost, to try to bandage the wound that forever shaped his relationship with his father.

"How did you feel when he said that?" I asked.

"I felt invisible, unwanted, unloved."

"What did you do?"

"I promised myself, right then and there, that if I ever had a child, he'd always know how much I loved him."

We hugged again and rested our heads on shoulders that were damp with tears.

"I never meant to spoil you . . . I always preached that other people have rights, too. You remember that, don't you? What I wanted most of all was for you to know how much I loved you."

I told Dad that, yes, I did remember, that he should remember that he had given me the most precious gift of all, the sense of being important. I loved him for that . . . and for everything else. He was unselfish, and from him I learned that true love is putting the other person's welfare before your own. Many years ago, when I was struggling with the decision to leave the newspaper in my hometown and go to Louisville, four hundred miles away, I asked Dad for his advice. I really was hesitant to leave home—a lot of only children are like this—and I expected that he would ask me to stay. What I actually said to him was "You don't think I should go, do you?" But he surprised me. Yes, he did think that I should go, that the opportunity was too great to pass up.

Years later he would discuss with me the agony behind that message. "It was the hardest thing I ever had to say. It was like I was dying inside, knowing I was helping you decide to move away. But it would have been selfish of me to suggest that you stay so we could see more of you and the grandchildren. To tie children to parents out of selfishness would be unpardonable. But even so, the temptation to do it is very great. We, your mother and I, had to fight it."

He was quite a guy. Yes, because of the wounds he suffered, he unknowingly helped to shape in me what at times came across as an exaggerated sense of my own importance, even a certain aloofness and swaggering. That was the negative side of it. But I never forget that there was another side, too. The sense of who I am, of my intrinsic worth, of my right to be where I am, has served me well. It is the foundation on which everything good has been erected.

And Then There Was Gregory

Gregory is a fifty-one-year-old businessman who was one of five children in a family that was short on nurturing, not because the parents lacked love but because they lacked the energy. His father was a policeman whose shift constantly was rotated, and, Gregory recalled, "he always seemed tired. When he worked nights, all he ever wanted to do was sleep, and when he worked days, he always wanted to rest to get ready for the nights." His mother worked in retail sales for long hours and low pay, and she, too, often was fatigued.

"They tried to pay attention to us, but it always was a contest among us kids to see who could get the most. As it turned out, we all lost, all of us, most of the time. 'Daddy, will you play catch with me?' 'Mommy, will you come and look at what I've drawn?' And they'd give us a minute or two, and that would be it. At times I thought I would die from my feelings of neglect, and sometimes I'd wonder why they had five children if they weren't going to spend time with us and help us to feel that we were worth something."

As an adult, Gregory still feels he must compete for attention, and that irritates some people, who feel he's pushy and arrogant and not very pleasant to be around.

Gregory decided many years ago that, if he married, he was going to have one child and that the child would know what it meant to be cared about. "I think parents can love their children and have the best intentions in the world but there's limited time and energy and if there are too many children, the children are going to feel shortchanged . . . and worthless."

How does Gregory feel he fared with his only child, a son who now is in his early twenties? "I think he knew that I always had time for him. I didn't always drop what I was doing, but . . ." Gregory suggested that I put the question to his son, and I did. The son had an answer that, when I shared it later with Gregory, figuratively caused him to pop his shirtbuttons.

"The thing about Dad was that I had the sense that he would drop whatever he was doing if I asked him for something. That made me feel important but, at the same time, it acted as an appropriate restraining mechanism for me. Because I knew I could get his attention, I wasn't always clamoring for it."

The people who work with Gregory's son feel that he, unlike his father, isn't always competing for attention. An associate told me: "When he asks for something, I know it's important, and I listen."

Love, Understanding, Frustration . . .

In this book I will share some of my experiences as an only child, but this is not primarily a personal book. Rather, it is what I consider a resource book for only children and those who in some intimate way interact with only children. While the experiences of which I and others speak are real, they may be different from the experiences of other people. It's not possible to say that everybody is this way or that way. There are valid generalizations that can be made, and there are exceptions to the generalizations.

In the final analysis, this is a book about love and understanding and frustration and fear and joy. It's a book about life.

Am I glad that I'm an only child? Yes, I am, even though after Mom died, I thought that I, too, might die. Of loneliness.

That Sunny Autumn Afternoon

It was during what would be my final visit with Mom. She and I sat on that marvelous front porch on a sunny autumn afternoon, and I asked if she and Dad had decided that I would be their only child.

Yes, she said, that decision had been made, after my birth. The pregnancy had occurred during the bleak years of the Great Depression, a time that was far from ideal for beginning a family, especially since Dad's job was on the line and extended unemployment was a distinct possibility.

The pregnancy was unplanned, she said, but she stressed, just as Dad had many years before: "Don't ever think that you weren't wanted. There's a big difference between being unplanned and being unwanted. Nobody ever loved a child more than we loved you."

Why had they decided against any more children? After all, she was one of three and he was one of five.

She and Dad had come from poor families, families that had known near-poverty at times, and they had agreed that it would be folly to have more mouths to feed and more minds to educate than they could afford. "After you arrived, we knew that was it because we'd be strapped to take care of you the way we wanted to."

They never had any regrets about it, she said. She and Dad liked having an only child, and I never displayed any of the negative qualities that commonly are pinned on only children—such as being selfish and ego-centered. When I told her I thought she was being overly generous, she wasn't deterred. They had loved me, she said, in a way that was wholehearted and without reservation. But they had done as much as was humanly possible to discourage me from thinking that I was Superman.

"How'd you do that?" I asked.

"By setting limits, by enforcing rules, by telling you when we thought you were out of line. We always tried to praise more than we criticized, but we didn't shy away from being critical when we thought it was appropriate. We wanted you to be the best person you could be."

I asked if she had been pleased with the way things turned out. She kissed me on the forehead, refilled my glass with champagne, smiled, looked into what had become a purple-tinged sunset and said that, yes, she was pleased. And proud.

The Words of Only Children

After Mom's death, I wrote a column about my last visit with her, and while I wasn't surprised that I heard from a number of only children, I was surprised by the passion and depth of feeling with which many of them expressed themselves.

Some of the letters looked at the down side of it:

"Your column rekindled feelings I thought I had conquered . . . When my father died three years ago, I was devastated. But then when my mother died, my feelings were much worse. Here I was, married for twenty years, mother of three daughters, and I could only think of myself as an orphan . . . It struck me with physical force that never again would anyone love me unconditionally, that no longer would I be the light of someone's life, that suddenly I was nobody's child . . . While growing up, I never minded my situation. I never was lonely because I learned that being alone was a natural, comfortable state. But I was not prepared for the loneliness and abandonment at my parents' deaths."

"Being an only child was, for me, a lonely experience. I had no experience . . . of learning how to be a friend to others, and in later years, this was painful for me. The give-and-take of family life with brothers and sisters would have helped me greatly. As I grew into adulthood, I felt the absence of siblings for another reason: I was the focus of all parental expectations. I felt a burden of responsibility to produce. I wasn't certain in what manner I should produce, but I experienced a sense of failure when I realized that I was unlikely to bring home any laurels for my parents . . . All their dreams were wrapped up in me."

"If an only child has any sense of responsibility, they experience the syndrome of 'all the eggs in one basket.' I had to be the best at school, sports and in my social life since all my parents' expectations were tied up in me . . . If the parents have a bad day, the only child gets the brunt of it . . . An only child can only dwell on what a terrible person he or she is . . . I'm still trying to be more flexible in my dealings with others. I have to work at not being possessive, jealous, and wanting my way to be *the* way. Fortunately, I have a strong husband."

"Ever since I can remember (I'm a teenager now), I have felt the constant pressure, usually unspoken, of high achievement. Because my parents always have supported me in anything I do and because I love them so much, I feel I have to overachieve to 'repay' them . . . Of course, I never reach these impossible goals, and I end up letting us all down. Since I'm the only child, I feel their success as parents depends on my success as a person."

"At times, in my growing-up years, I longed for siblings. I really didn't always enjoy constantly being the center of my parents' attention. I felt as if I had to struggle to carve out private time to read in my room without hurting their feelings."

Other letters looked at the positive side of being an only child:

"I always have been glad that I am an only child. I have found that I usually have no discomfort with being alone and in fact often prefer it, although I enjoy being with others, too. I have always felt that learning to value my own company and having time to think through problems alone were among the great benefits of being an only child . . . If my wife and I planned to have children, I think that having 'just one' would be a strong possibility. Perhaps that is really the final measure of the experience."

"As an only child, I grew up in relative solitude, which I learned to savor. Perhaps a benchmark of good mental health is being comfortable with oneself and, as an only child, I certainly cherish this advantage over those who so often seem to be wringing their hands and wondering what to do with their time."

"Because I am an only child, I grew up with a good measure of confidence in myself because my parents, in all ways, made me feel that I was an exceptional person. In my adult life I've faced my share of reversals, and I've not crumbled, not even in situations in which some other people fell by the wayside. I believe my confidence and self-love, instilled by parents who poured all their attention and affection into me, have made it possible for me to be a survivor, in the most positive sense of the word."

"I felt pressure to make the most of my abilities, and this is supposed to be a negative factor for only children. It's what is supposed to turn them into driven perfectionists. But it didn't affect me that way, probably because my parents never caused me to think that if I didn't win every time out, they wouldn't love me. No, the baseline of love was always there, a given, a constant. And I responded to that. I wanted them to be proud of me, and they were."

"Sometimes I wonder what it would be like to have a brother or a sister, but in truth I'm happy to be an only child. My parents didn't overvalue me, as you read about with some only children, but they certainly made me aware of how important I was to them. It's nice to be the center of attention. I thrive on that, even today, and it's probably a major reason why I've done so well in corporate life. It's given me the incentive to put myself into positions where I could be the focal point."

A Reason to Celebrate

When Gary Foster was a student at Wittenberg University in the early 1970s, he developed close relationships with two other students, and eventually the three of them shared an apartment. "We recognized a lot of similar qualities in each other. We had a lot in common." The bond they shared was that they were only children, and at times they felt alone in a world in which everybody else seemed to have brothers and sisters who telephoned, wrote letters and in other ways conveyed their love, interest, and concern.

"We spent a lot of time talking about growing up by ourselves, and we decided we were going to compensate for not being from large families. We formed an Only Child Club, starting with the three of us and eventually we expanded to eight people. It was a fun thing, and it gave us a bond that other people had with brothers and sisters."

There was a special handshake for members only. "You'd extend the index finger to the other person's wrist and cover it up with your left hand. All fraternities had their own handshakes, and we wanted ours, too." The club's colors were red and green, just like Christmas, said Foster, because "every day is Christmas for an only child . . . As only children, we tended to get more things growing up than children from larger families. None of us ever hurt for anything. We'd never been deprived. To us the Christmas colors were symbolic of what it was to be an only child."

That was the jolly part of it, said Foster, who today is married, the father of two children, a safety/health specialist for ICI Pharmaceuticals Group in Newark, Delaware. The down side, as he grew into adulthood, was the realization that, without siblings, he had "missed the obligation to learn how to share better. I never had to share anything. People later pointed out that they recognized this was a problem for me. It was hard to hear that, but, as I look back, I have to agree. I never shared a bedroom, a car, my parents' attention. Now I may overshare to compensate, and people have talked to me about this, too."

Foster said he felt important growing up and he still feels important, a quality he recognizes "in the other only children I meet. They are all disciplined; they do well in society. They are very aggressive, in a positive way, and I've not met an only child I felt was not well-suited for the environment." Foster is able to identify an only child very quickly. "I can work with somebody for as little as a day, and I know. There's something about the way they carry themselves, the confidence . . . It has something to do with how we handle work and personal affairs, the independence, the intense attention to task."

Some Thoughts on Only Children

Paul J. Fink, president of the American Psychiatric Association in 1988, is married to an only child, and "I listen to her talk about how she and her parents would sit around the table at dinner, as equals, and discuss current events and politics. At my house there always was a ruckus by the kids that made it impossible to talk about anything in a normal way. There's a great opportunity for the only child to be 'adultified.' This can be good or bad. In terms of learning, it can be very good. But if the only child is overstimulated, expected to do things beyond his years, it can be bad."

Psychologist William Liberi: "I never minded being an only child. In fact, I liked it. There are some tremendous advantages. I was the center of attention; nobody got in my way; a lot of love was lavished on me."

Psychiatrist Alan Summers: "If you just want a happy life, don't be an only child. But if you want to achieve, create, have interesting experiences, reach your potential, then you should be an only child. Being an only child gives you a greater chance of moving toward your potential. I'm always in a striving state."

Psychologist Maurice Prout: "I would choose to be an only child all over again. Why? Because the only child gets the whole pie, and I enjoyed the whole pie. As I got older and acquired some scar tissue, I realized that I couldn't always have the whole pie in the outside world, but I wouldn't trade what I got from being an only child."

Child psychiatrist Henri Parens: "The only child can be made a prince by the parents . . . or a frog. Being a prince has problems as well as assets, but there's no question that the only child who is made a frog is going to suffer greatly. All of the mud is dumped on this one frog, and he won't have siblings to turn to for support and to share the misery."

Frederic F. Flach, psychiatrist, successful author and only child: "The only child has no brothers and sisters to identify with so he forms a strong identification with his parents. He has more ambition to grow up."

The down side of this is that the only child may become insecure because he can't compete successfully with his parents. Yet this insecurity may be responsible for much achievement because the only child tends to work harder to compensate for his feelings of insecurity.

Another way in which the only child compensates is by trying to be perfect.

Ah, yes. Perfectionism. That's something I know a little bit about.

— 2 —

The Demon Perfectionism

For a long time I've recognized that I have been dogged by perfectionism, that I never would crack the whip on somebody else quite the way I crack it on myself when I fall short of my own expectations. I've talked about it, joked about it, made fun of the craziness of it. Maybe that's the price, I'd say, of being an only child. But my recognition was intellectual. Emotionally, I didn't understand until . . .

It was a cold, rainy afternoon in late fall at our beach place in Delaware, and it seemed like a good time to put light dimmers in the master bedroom and the living room. Over the years I've put in maybe a dozen dimmers in houses I've owned, and, believe me, it's not a big deal. You just splice in the wires and, presto, you're in business.

So I drove to the hardware store and bought two dimmers. Then I unscrewed the switch plate and pulled the electrical switch out of its box in the bedroom. What I saw puzzled me. The switch was connected by four wires. Not two, as I had expected, not even three, which is what you find when you're working with a light that can be controlled from two locations.

What would I do with four wires? Well, it couldn't be all that difficult. I'd cap the white wire, and I'd hook up the red one and the two black ones. I did it, flipped the power back on and, ah, yes, the dimmer worked. But my wife, Marilyn, who was reading in the living room, wondered out loud why the stereo had gone dead.

I felt frustrated, but, not to worry, I was equal to the task. I'd rewire, and then everything would be all right. I rewired, and the stereo blared forth, but now the dimmer didn't work. I rewired again, but I couldn't get the dimmer and the stereo to work at the same time.

Now I was more than frustrated. I was angry. I nearly was in a rage. I stormed into the kitchen and fixed a stiff drink—bourbon, ice, very little water. I gulped that down, fixed another one. I wondered why I was so distressed. Plainly, I was overreacting. But why? The worst that could happen was that I'd have to call an electrician, but I was furious. I started a conversation with myself.

"Why am I in such a funk?"

"You couldn't fix the light, you dummy."

"Why is that a big deal?"

"You ought to be able to fix it."

"Why should I ought to be able to fix it? I'm not an electrician."

"You just should, that's why. After all, you're Darrell Sifford."

"What's that got to do with it?"

"Everything, dummy. Darrell Sifford can do anything. He's perfect."

I heard myself say those words, and I couldn't believe it. "He's perfect." I poured yet another drink, invited Marilyn to join me at the dining room table and then let the memories of yesteryear come tumbling out.

I was a senior in high school, captain of the football team, the all-star end who caught everything within reach and some things that were out of reach. Before every game, I vomited from nervousness, usually in the locker room but sometimes right out on the field.

On this night I did it in the locker room, and, as I came out of the stall, the team physician, the father of our best running back, put his arm around my shoulders and asked:

"What's the matter, son?"

"I'm afraid I'll make a mistake."

"Would that be so awful?"

"It would be for me."

I was seventeen, and a mistake was unacceptable . . . because I had to be perfect.

We played the biggest high school in Missouri, an awesome team in bright red jerseys, and we won, 13–12. I caught a touchdown pass and threw the downfield block that cut the doctor's son loose for the other touchdown. But something unheard of happened in that game. I dropped a pass.

I came back to the huddle and somebody asked "What happened?" I was embarrassed and mad enough to bite nails. I told the quarterback to throw it to me again. He did, and I caught it for a big gain.

Then the game was over. The upset had happened. The crowd, in joyous disbelief, took over the field, and the coach was hugging me.

"Mack," I said to him, "I'm sorry about the pass I dropped."

"Hell, we beat 'em. You were great!"

"I dropped a pass."

I was seventeen, and even then I wondered why I couldn't savor the victory with my teammates. It was, of course, because I had been imperfect.

I was thirty-two, well into my newspaper career, with visions of greatness dancing in my head. Dad and I were having dinner at a steakhouse, just the two of us, and I was telling him how far I was going to go.

"How many people," he asked, "get to where you're talking about? One in a thousand? One in ten thousand? How many?"

I was hurt, and I was angry. "I don't care about that. I'll be the one!"

Why was I hurt and angry? Because Dad, the most important man in my life, had questioned my perfectionism. If he really loved me, how could he do this to me?

I sat there and sobbed . . . and Marilyn listened with compassion and patience . . . I recalled other stories, one after another. There it was, all out on the table, in all its ugliness, and for the first time

I felt it. Emotionally, I felt the pain of trying to be perfect. I thought about the damage that it had caused me and those I loved, about the times, when my own sons were growing up, that I had been unwilling to accept less than perfection from them, and how I had reacted when I didn't get perfection. I thought about the people who had worked for me, when I was a newspaper editor. I thought about my first wife. I thought about Marilyn. I thought about . . . I poured yet another drink because the pain at times felt life-threatening. But then it passed, and a sense of peace replaced the pain. I felt relieved, cleansed, as if I had been reborn. I stopped sobbing and wiped my eyes. Now I really did understand, and I wouldn't have to be like that anymore. I wouldn't have to expect the impossible. It was, it seemed, the ultimate catharsis.

Over lunch, not long after that, I told my story to psychologist Daniel Gottlieb, who's been a friend for many years. He understood. There's a little bit of the perfectionist in a lot of us, he said, and a lot of it in some of us, especially in only children.

I told him about my plans for the coming weekend, and he told me to "have a good weekend. A good, imperfect weekend."

I've worked hard at having not only imperfect weekends but also imperfect days, hours, minutes, seconds. And it has been hard work, giving myself permission to mess up, relaxing my standard to the point that I can tell myself—and believe—that it really doesn't matter. In the long run, in the big picture, it truly doesn't matter.

And, I'm convinced, this is what it takes for a perfectionist to break out of the pattern: permission. It's the greatest gift that anybody can give to himself because it's the most freeing thing on earth.

Yes, It Can Be Discouraging

In *The Birth Order Book* (1985) psychologist Kevin Leman devoted a chapter to what he called a "prescription for discouraged perfectionists." Here is some of what he wrote:

"Realize that perfection is a deadly enemy. I call it 'slow suicide.' Only children are the worst offenders, followed by first-borns . . . To control your perfectionism, you must recognize your desperate need to be perfect. Not only that, you must recognize the fallacy and futility in this kind of thinking. You are never going to be perfect. Why not give yourself permission to be imperfect?

"Make a conscious effort to go easy on criticizing yourself and others . . . When others criticize, don't be so quick to react . . . Be aware of your sensitivity . . . Perfectionists aren't known for being forgiving. In fact, when insulted or unappreciated, they can nurse grudges for far too long. Do you need to work on your ability to grant forgiveness? For the perfectionist, the key to forgiveness lies in realizing that people make mistakes and the world still goes on."

What's It All About, Anyway?

Yes, indeed, the world still goes on. It's important to realize that, for the most part, the stuff we flap about is not worth the flapping. It's important not to sweat the small stuff . . . and to realize that it's not really important at all.

Is this easier said than done? Yes, it is. We have a special burden, the only children of the world, and it is that we must please our parents. This is a point on which therapists are in broad agreement—because they see so many only children whose problems are rooted in it. The only child's mandate to please may have come in response to parental messages that were interpreted, rightly or wrongly, to mean "We will love you and nurture you—as long as you make us happy." In other cases, the parents didn't give out any such message at all, but the only child figured it out for himself: "I'm all they've got, so it's my responsibility to make them proud of me." What is the surest way to make parents proud and happy? By being perfect, naturally.

Psychologist Carol Gantman, who is the mother of an only child, said: "The only child thinks his job is to please the parents, and we, as parents, sort of promote that. It's how we teach them to behave: 'Do this and I'll be happy.' Or it could be much more subtle: 'When you're with us, we're a happy family.' Only children are very sensitive and pick up cues from parents." Some parents may not even be aware of how they are nudging their child toward perfectionism.

And so, for whatever reason, only children get hooked and begin the chase for the holy grail of perfectionism. We can't ever reach it, of course, but that doesn't stop us from trying . . . and trying. Psychiatrist Pirooz Sholevar, the father of an only child, said it's a struggle that seems unending to convince the only child that enough is enough. "Hey, you're okay. I love you. You don't have to *do* anything else. I'm happy with you the way you are."

Understanding why we're the way we are is helpful. Having around us people who understand is helpful, too. But our special craziness probably never goes away completely. I slip back into my old ways every now and then, and probably I always will. When I falter, I forgive myself, and I try to laugh. For me that's progress.

And Then There Was George

Her name is Thelma, and she's puzzled about something that's vitally important to her husband, George, who is an only child. She's puzzled because it seems so silly to her. George works near Dallas and lives in an apartment, while Thelma works in Baltimore and lives in their home there. Twice a month she flies to Texas to spend long weekends with George. The trouble starts when she walks in the front door of the apartment.

"I'm not allowed to make tracks on his freshly vacuumed carpet. He likes to see those marks from the vacuum cleaner, and he gets furious if I walk on the carpet. So what do I do? I tiptoe around the edges, near the baseboard, and that's okay with him. Is this nutty? Well, maybe it is, but it keeps him happy, so what does it matter? I hope that someday we get to the point where we can joke about this, but we're not there yet."

George said that he didn't see anything unusual about his passion for clean carpets. "My mother made a big deal about my keeping my room spotless. It angered me if kids came upstairs and messed it up, so why should it be any different with my wife? Why is it so hard for her to understand that?"

. . . And Some Other People, Too

Some other only children have told me about their own perfectionist tendencies.

Jerry said that he drives his wife crazy because he's always picking up after her. "She's always drinking half of her cup of coffee and leaving the cup in the kitchen sink. I go in, dump out the coffee, rinse the cup and put it in the dishwasher. Why do I do that? I don't know. I used to mention it every time it happened. I'd say to Sally, 'Well, dear, I just put your coffee cup away.' And finally one day she exploded and told me what I could do with her coffee cup. Since then, I've stopped mentioning it to her, but I still pick up after her. I can't stop doing it. If everything's not perfect in the house, I can't be relaxed."

A college professor said that it takes him forever and a day to prepare a lecture because he insists on perfection in his outline. "I used to not worry about this but now, in midlife, I'm unwilling to accept anything but the very best. So now I rewrite and rewrite, and I end up taking ten hours to do something that a normal person could do in two hours. I just can't turn it loose."

A businessman said that his perfectionism had turned him into a procrastinator. He's fearful that what he does won't be perfect, so he delays doing it. It has cost him some business, he said, but he hasn't been able to change. "I wish to hell I could tell myself 'I'm going to do the best I can do at this time with what I have to work with, and that's it.' But I just won't do that, and so I sit and stew and feel miserable about myself and my work."

A housewife said that she cleans her two bathrooms from top to bottom every single day and polishes the faucets until they sparkle. She complains bitterly to her husband and the kids when they leave fingerprints on the handles of the faucets. "They think this is sort of crazy, and in a way it is. If a bathroom isn't to be used, what's it for? I understand that, but it's important to me that my bathrooms be perfectly clean, and I'm irritated if somebody messes them up."

A businesswoman told me that she's forever late for the office because it takes her hours to get ready. Hours? Yes, she said, it takes hours even though she considers herself to be well organized. Every night she lays out the next day's clothing on the sofa, but then, come morning, nothing looks right when she puts it on, and always she finds herself trying on two or three different things and fussing about the right shoes and handbag. "I feel silly telling you about this, and you must think that I'm a person who lacks self-confidence, otherwise why would looking just right be so essential? But I don't consider myself short on confidence. At the office I make decisions that affect the business and other people, and I don't spend a lot of time second-guessing myself . . . But how I present myself is something else."

A student told me he'd dropped out of college because he chose not to do the work rather than run the risk of doing it imperfectly. The psychiatrist to whom he went eventually for help, Alan Summers, said that the student's action was not uncommon for perfectionistic only children. "As long as you don't do something, you always can tell yourself that if you had done it, it would have been perfect. And you can keep that illusion as long as you don't do it. It's like the guy who says that if he played golf regularly, he'd get good enough to beat Arnold Palmer . . . He can think that as long as he doesn't permit himself to play regularly."

Summers said that people who are heavily invested in perfection tend to burn out emotionally much quicker than those who are more realistic and less demanding. Often, he said, they get caught up in insignificant details, spin their wheels and accomplish very little. Instead of being perfect, which is their goal, they end up at the other end of the spectrum and never understand what happened to them.

Who Are They and What Do They Want?

Rosemarie Deering is an educational psychologist at Kansas State University with a special interest in perfectionism and only children. She became an only child at eight when her six-year-old sister died. "My childhood ended that night," she said, as she struggled to comfort her parents and be perfect to make up for their loss. She grew up, went to college, taught school for thirty-five years and, in her words, "readily identified many other perfectionistic students for whom their perfectionism was a problem,"

bright children who didn't seem to realize their potential because
. . . "The perfectionistic only child seems so often to engage in
all-or-nothing thinking. It's difficult for them to think in terms of
moderation. It's perfect or it's nothing. They rarely perceive
things as being perfect, so then things are seen as dastardly." This
is part of the reason some of them struggle. They give up because
they can't be perfect.

After she left teaching, Deering completed work on her doctoral
degree and then developed two strategies to help identify perfectionists. One is for teachers to evaluate elementary-age children,
"not to try to change them from being perfectionistic but to help
teachers adopt strategies that will be helpful to the children
. . . What teachers need to do is focus on the socialization experience, on learning goals instead of performance goals, on increasing
cooperation and lessening competition. I'm opposed to reading
groups that are labeled Eagles and Crows and things like that.
Somebody who's called a Crow can carry that around as a deficit
all of his life . . . Perfectionists do better with approval. Everybody
does, but especially the perfectionist."

Deering's second strategy is a self-report for college students,
some of whom are functioning far below their potential. "They're
making passing grades, and so nobody pays too much attention to
them, but I have a sense that they may be the unidentified victims
of perfectionism. They're not perceived as failures but they're not
identified as gifted, and some of them potentially are gifted. It's
just that they're immobilized to some extent by their perfectionism . . . Some of them eventually drop out of school . . . Many
juvenile delinquents, I'm convinced, are our heroes gone astray."

One Man's (Losing) Battle against Perfectionism

What does corporate America think about perfectionism? Psychologist Arnold Lazarus of Rutgers University got a firsthand
lesson that was painful. Lazarus, who was named one of the ten
most influential psychotherapists in America in a survey published
in *American Psychologist,* gives a large number of workshops and
seminars to executives at some of the nation's biggest and best-
known corporations. One of those corporations fired him a while

back because the people at the top didn't like the message that he was bringing to the workplace.

What was that message? It's not necessary to be perfect. "In conducting a series of seminars on stress reduction and coping skills, I was emphasizing a point that I regard as essential. In essence, I was attacking the notion that one should strive for excellence and perfection. I pointed out that by continuously trying to produce nothing short of excellence, the strain would be enormous, and burnout would be almost inevitable. Instead, I argued that adequacy was to be the ongoing goal. By adequacy, I did not mean a bare average performance but rather a level of proficiency that was far better than average. When aiming for adequacy, as I defined it, one might fairly often perform excellently, whereas a perfectionistic outlook might tend to undermine excellent output due to the strains imposed by the excessive demands placed upon oneself . . . In keeping with this, I added another piece of stress-reduction wisdom. I stated that to always try to be the best or even to be at your best is unrealistic. Situations often arise that make it virtually impossible to give of one's best. One may be under the weather, out of sorts, worried or distracted by some important event in life. You can try to do your best under the circumstances, and you can endeavor to ensure that your output is adequate, but it is important to resist demands from oneself and from others always to give a perfect 100 percent."

The corporate audiences, Lazarus told me, received this philosophy enthusiastically, but when news of the lectures "got to the higher-ups in the corporation, I was summoned to meet with some of them. They proceeded to tell me that their credo was 'strive for excellence' and that their employees were urged, at all times, to aim for nothing less than 120 percent. I was told to drop the message to strive for adequacy. I argued that their credo would guarantee undue levels of stress, unhealthy competition, and would have several other unfortunate side-effects. I added that my adequacy philosophy, far from undermining productivity, producing sloppy work or encouraging second-rate service, actually would increase morale and result in better work and happier employees." So what happened? "The rest of my seminars were duly canceled. The reason provided was that suddenly this billion-dollar corporation had run into budget problems."

I asked Lazarus to talk more about what he considers the price extracted by constantly trying to be perfect. He said that books devoted to the pursuit of excellence often become best-sellers, "yet this perfectionistic bias is probably at the core of most stress-related problems," including high blood pressure, coronary disease, ulcers, asthma, headaches, depression, alcoholism and drug abuse. "As long as presidents and upper managers of large corporations keep pushing their personnel beyond the breaking point, refusing to listen to reason and simply firing people who try to offer an outlook that works, I pity the employees who fall into their traps."

Lazarus said the pursuit of perfection "does not allow for the human frailties that exist. You have a bad day, and you can't give your best. If you've got to give your best anyway, if the show must go on, then you're under tremendous strain, and your system gets overloaded. But even if you're under the weather, you may be able to give a better-than-average performance. You keep a little in reserve for yourself, so you don't die on stage. The whole attitude is one in which the dignity of the individual is maintained instead of sacrificing everything for the organization. This is a self-destruct mode for corporations."

In Lazarus's view, there are some people who are "like race-horses, and you can't ask a racehorse to be a cart horse. They thrive on the fast pace, and they should never marry, because they're so career-oriented. They can work seventy or eighty hours a week and love it. But if somebody who's not built that way is asked to emulate the racehorse, that person could die. For the vast majority, trying to be perfect and to give 120 percent will be destructive."

Has Anybody Seen an Exit?

What is the way out of the box for perfectionists? What can we do to recognize the need for some breathing space and to build that into our lives?

I think we can recognize ourselves for what we are—people

who rather consistently expect the impossible of ourselves—and make a plan for change. One thing that can be helpful is to set up situations in which we're likely not to succeed, so we can get some experience at failing. Perfectionists, for the most part, don't have much practice at coming up short. We need to know we can foul up and that, in the long run, it won't rock the boat. At least not very much.

Tug McGraw, the Phillies' legendary relief pitcher, supposedly originated what is popularly called "the frozen snowball theory," and it's something that perfectionistic only children might keep in mind. The story, which allegedly came about because reporters always were asking McGraw how he could enter games in pressure situations night after night and not eventually fold, goes like this:

Slowly, millions of years from now, the earth will begin to drift out of orbit around the sun, and, as a result, the earth's temperature will drop and drop until at some point the earth will resemble a giant frozen snowball. When this happens, will anybody remember if Tug McGraw won or lost tonight's game? Will anybody care?

Will anybody care if the faucet handles were clean of fingerprints, if the carpets were without footprints, if the handbag matched the shoes, if the half-filled coffee cup remained in the kitchen sink?

Ozymandias, Where Are You?

It helps all of us not to take ourselves too seriously, to be able to laugh at ourselves, but it especially helps the perfectionistic only child. There's a sonnet, written in 1817 by Percy Bysshe Shelley, the English poet, that makes the point more eloquently than anything I know. The title is "Ozymandias," the Greek name for Ramses II, who was the pharaoh of Egypt with whom Moses contended during the Exodus. This powerful piece of work, only fourteen lines long, tells of a wrecked statue in the desert. The shattered face lies nearby, displaying a "frown, and wrinkled lip, and sneer of cold command." The last lines are these:

> And on the pedestal, these words appear:
> "My name is Ozymandias, king of kings:

Look on my works, ye Mighty, and despair!"
Nothing beside remains. Round the decay
Of that colossal wreck, boundless and bare,
The lone and level sands stretch far away.

It's a poem that psychiatrist Richard Moscotti sometimes reads to those who come to him for help. "In my therapy sessions with people, as we discuss their problems and relevant life issues, a subject that often arises is how to survive the pain and trauma, irony and defeat, that is sometimes out there for all of us. This frequently leads to a discussion of the importance of perspective and balance in one's life . . . Shelley's poem tells me that nothing is forever, that it's important to keep your view of the big picture and the little picture balanced. What I tell people is to remember, you're the center of your own world, but you're only one-five-billionth of the people on the planet. Don't believe 100 percent of your own flowery press clippings. Don't be pompous. Don't be so serious about yourself and what you're doing . . . Can you imagine Ozymandias telling a joke? Laughing riotously? Neither can I . . . If we all could laugh at ourselves more, the world would be the better for it."

"Ozymandias syndrome" is Moscotti's name for the people who, like Ozymandias, "miss the forest for the trees and get their priorities messed up about what's important . . . I'm seeing an extremely successful business executive, an only child, who entered therapy to attempt to clarify some disquieting existential issues . . . and a subtle feeling of missing somehow the joy of living. When he heard Shelley's poem, he quickly identified with Ozymandias and recognized his own imperiousness as a defense and distancing mechanism. Although highly efficient in the business world, he had a style that did damage to the more gentle interpersonal relationships at home. He even nicknamed himself 'Ozzie' during those times when he slipped back into his earlier pattern as the 'king.' In overthrowing his 'sneer of cold command,' he has found greatly increased love and happiness in his family and friends. The world notices and likes the change."

I asked Moscotti what we can do when we discover—or when others tell us—that we're swimming in pomposity that would do justice to a king.

"Try to get outside of yourself and see yourself the way others see you. I once got caught in a blizzard in New Jersey, and it was like the world could end if I didn't get to where I needed to be. It was five o'clock in the morning, and I waded into the parking lot, found my car, which looked like a lump in the snow, and then I shoveled it out and got to the highway. There were no other cars, and I was speeding down the highway, driving like hell, and I looked at the speedometer . . . and I was going 15 miles an hour. I broke up laughing, made a U-turn and went back to town, which was only about a mile away . . . I think that's what we have to do—be aware of the vicissitudes of life and be prepared to laugh."

The Ozymandias story has helped me deal with my perfectionism. So have some other things. I have a saying that I utter to myself, and anybody within earshot, when I begin to feel bogged down, too serious, too buried in the business of life: "Mostly it's junk." It's a reminder that, for the most part, the things that I get in a flap about aren't worth it. At other times I take down from my office bulletin board and read from the anonymously written essay *I'd Pick More Daisies*. My favorite part is this:

> "If I had my life to live over, I'd start barefooted in the spring and stay that way later in the fall. I'd play hooky more. I wouldn't make such good grades, except by accident . . . I'd eat more ice cream and less beans . . . I'd ride on more merry-go-rounds . . . And I'd pick more daisies."

If I'm at the beach, I focus on the crashing surf, try to count the whitecaps, watch the dolphins at play, anticipate the moon's coming up like an orange ball on the water, put on a Rossini tape that reminds me that life is robust and meant to be lived, joyfully . . . but not perfectly—except by accident.

Where There's Balance, There's Life

When we're caught up in the serious business of trying to be perfect, when we're in pain, we need to stop and examine our lives. Most of the time we'll find that we've lost our balance and, like the dancer on the high wire, we're in danger of taking a spill. I have a friend who swears by what he calls the "life balance quotient," which consists of four qualities that are tied to working, loving and playing. Those of us who are able to do reasonably well in these four areas tend to lead satisfying lives and to have fewer regrets than everybody else. Here are the four qualities:

The ability to work. Underworking is bad, and it's devastating when we don't scratch the surface of our potential, but overworking can kill. I can testify to that. Overworking can kill the love that we have for others and for ourselves and can deaden the soul. For many, work is an avoidance mechanism, an anesthetic against the agony of a life out of control. They stay at work to avoid the greatest work of all—the effort required to cope with family dynamics and interpersonal relationships. For many it's easier to overwork than to come home and face the music, easier than trying to change the music. We should enjoy what we do, because we spend so much time and energy doing it, but we shouldn't allow it to become the master of our lives. In the long run, it really doesn't mean that much. This is what behaviorist Andrew Salter obviously had in mind when he said that he'd never met anybody who, on his deathbed, wished that he had spent more time at work.

The ability to love. Most of us have this capacity if we've had some degree of good parenting, especially good mothering, and some nurturing adult figures in childhood. In fact, most of us *need* to love, but often we find ourselves loving not wisely and not well. Often the love we have for another person is obsessive, neurotic, dependent, irrational. In a way, love can be dangerous because to truly love, we must make ourselves vulnerable to the other person. This is where a lot of people hedge their bets.

The ability to be loved. It's amazing, and downright tragic, how many people feel unworthy of love. It's a problem that therapists encounter daily. The more insecure a person is, the less that person feels worthy of being loved.

A feeling of worthiness, of being loved, starts very early in our development. The more healthy parenting we get as children, the more nurturing we can give and receive later in life. This is where the only child potentially is far ahead of the pack because of the greater possibility of getting so much undiluted love.

The ability to play. All of us need time to recharge our batteries.

A proper balance between work and play is mandatory, and to people whose work ethic threatens to destroy them, I would suggest that they give themselves the job of *not* having a job so they can learn to play. Some people can't let go of work and enjoy time off. They go on vacation and it's "Relax, 2-3-4, Relax, 2-3-4." They *work* at relaxing, which, of course, defeats the purpose. I think we need to ask ourselves two questions: What is fun for me? Why don't I do more of it?

I posed those questions in a speech at a meeting of all-male business executives, and a man in the back of the auditorium hollered: "I know what's fun, but my wife won't let me do it!" Everybody roared, but the truth of the matter is that it's not the spouse or the boss or the corporation that won't let us have fun. We do it to ourselves, and in that sense we truly are our own worst enemies, just as Pogo once proclaimed: "We have met the enemy and he is us."

Psychologist Arnold Lazarus said, on hearing of the death of a friend, "I hope he had enough fun." Not enough money. Not enough power. Not enough windows in the corner office—but enough fun. We need to recapture the enthusiasm of that little child who lives within us and who never dies, no matter how deeply we bury him. We need to let him come out and show us how to play. We need to learn to be as we once were, little children.

And Another Thing . . .

I think there's something else we can do, too. We can learn how to depersonalize failure and our lack of perfection. We need to focus on what we've learned from the experience. As psychologist Philip Bobrove said: "In that sense, looking at what we've learned, there is no such thing as failure. If we can say 'Man, I'll never make that dumb mistake again,' then we have grown. We learn from our mistakes, not from our successes."

Not all only children are perfectionistic, of course. On the surface some seem to be exactly the opposite. When I talked about perfectionism with Marcia, an only child who is forty-three, she shrugged and said she couldn't identify with it. "If you told my mother that I was a perfectionist, she'd die laughing. As a kid, I was messy, and my room always looked like a disaster."

Yes, it's that way for some only children, the flip side of perfectionism. They're rebelling against their parents or the world or whatever, and this is the form that their rebellion takes. The same dynamic is at work; it's merely acted out in a different way.

. . . One More Story

For many of us, until we learn better, the demon perfectionism provides the cadence to which we march and march and . . . Let me tell you another story:

The boy was eight years old, and he was fascinated by airplanes. Quite naturally he began to build models of his favorite planes, mostly World War II fighters. He was very good at building models, everybody told him that—but he never was quite satisfied. They never were good enough, and even though he hung them from the ceiling of his bedroom, he always wanted to make better models, perfect models.

Once, he finished a model of a Messerschmidt-109 and there was something different about the way he felt. He held it in his hands and, for the first time, he was thrilled with what he saw. It was . . . perfect. Perfect in every detail. He had done it, finally, and he felt that he, too, was perfect, like the model.

He brought it to his mother because he knew she would be so pleased. When he returned with it to his room, he watched in horror as his yellow cat, Sandy, playfully pounced on the plane. A front claw punctured the plane's tissue-paper skin, and the boy screamed in anguish.

He picked up the plane, tears of rage and disappointment flowing down his cheeks, and he crushed it . . . along with all the weeks of painstaking effort that had gone into it.

"Why'd you do that?" his mother asked.

"Because Sandy ruined it," the boy answered. "It wasn't perfect anymore."

The mother hugged her sad little boy. "I liked it. I thought it was perfect enough."

Perfect enough. Yes, of course, that's the answer. But I didn't

understand that when I was eight and holding the broken Mes-
serschmidt in my hands, and I didn't understand it for years and
years after that, when I called myself an adult yet at times led a
confused life because of my perfectionism and workaholism.

But we can learn. We can change. That's the good news.

3

Battling the
Obsessive-Compulsive Dragon

Louise was thirty-six. Her first child had been born recently, and this was a special evening because she and her husband were going out without the baby for the first time since their return from the hospital.

"My mother had come over to babysit, and she was in the living room when I came down the stairs, so excited about going to the movies. She looked up at me and, in that tone of voice she so often used when I was little, she said: 'Louise, you're not going to wear *those* shoes, are you?' Automatically, I responded 'Of course not,' and turned and ran back to the bedroom to change." It was a conditioned reflex, because Louise was programmed to deliver what mother wanted. That's how it always had been, and Louise hated it. But what could she do about it at this late date?

Now forty-two and with the scrubbed good looks of a college cheerleader, Louise talked about the heavy load of living her life trying to please her mother. She was six months old when she was adopted by middle-aged parents, who seemed determined that their only child would be everything they wanted her to be. Their attitude drove Louise into obsessive behavior that nearly destroyed her life.

"My father was an absentee father. He traveled a lot on business, and I can't recall that I ever had a meaningful conversation with him . . . My mother was the primary care-giver, very impatient, demanding, compulsive about cleanliness . . . I grew up with such social anxiety. She always was comparing me with other children, and I couldn't hold a flag to any of them . . . That's supposed to be one of the good things about being an only child—not being compared always to brothers and sisters—but that didn't stop my mother. She compared me to my friends and cousins . . . When I blushed, and I blushed often, she always pointed it out. 'Louise, why are you blushing? What's wrong with you?' I developed a phobia about blushing . . . I began to avoid social situations, and by the time I was fifteen, I was abusing alcohol to lessen my anxiety."

One of the messages she continually received from her mother was that "it was good to be thin, and it was bad to be anything but thin." Louise was a gaunt 117 pounds when she went away to college, but there, subjected to social pressures that prompted her to drink even more heavily, she scaled up to 150 pounds. Certainly she was not fat—she was five feet seven—but her mother railed at her to lose weight. "She was so concerned with how I looked; she was absolutely unconcerned with how I felt."

Straight out of college, Louise married for what she later would describe as all the wrong reasons, but marriage didn't bridle her mother's criticism. "My mother always told me I had fat arms. Rationally, I knew my arms weren't fat, but I'd look in the mirror, and, incredibly, my arms would look fat to me." One morning, as she stood in the kitchen munching some dry cornflakes, it occurred to her that "if I want to eat all I want but not gain weight," she could induce vomiting immediately after eating.

The year was 1970, and the nightmare was beginning. For fifteen years, she lived in anxiety, fear, dread and shame—as she gulped down food and vomited it, sometimes three or four times a day. In the years that followed, she ended her first marriage, remarried and had two children, but her horrible ritual continued and nobody ever knew.

"I remember the day I was almost found out. I had prepared a tremendously large bowl of pasta and I stuffed it down . . . and then I vomited, and just as I finished, somebody knocked on the door. My eyes were bloodshot, my face was flushed, and I was extremely nervous, filled with guilt and remorse. I opened the door, and it was a friend's husband. He wanted permission to cut some firewood on the property. I thought 'Surely he'll know what I've done,' but there was no indication that he suspected anything."

Louise started running compulsively. "I was running every day, at least four miles, sometimes eight or ten miles. The running seemed to decrease my vomiting episodes because I had something else to rely on for weight control."

But for the most part the ritual continued. "It's not the amount of food you eat," Louise says, "but how you eat it. You wolf it down. You don't enjoy it. You're in an anxiety-laden state."

One day, she read a magazine article entitled "Good Girls' Disease," about women who binged and vomited. It terrified her because "it was like it made my secret public." Then, in 1985, there was a television show that she tuned in to quite by accident, a show about perfection-oriented women who binged and vomited. They had a disorder called bulimia, which nobody knew much about. A few days later she saw a newspaper advertisement that carried the headline "Bulimia: Do you need help?"

Louise decided that she did need help. "I was disgusted, and I wanted to get rid of it. I was nervous and didn't feel confident. I didn't want to live any longer like that. I was thirty-nine and felt like such a jerk."

The therapist with whom Louise was matched at a center that treated eating disorders was Theresa Forrest, who over the years has worked with numbers of only children.

"What I see again and again is the child who is viewed by the parents in a certain way—with Louise it was that she wasn't good enough and didn't compare favorably with other children. The problem that the only child has is that there's nobody around to check out things with, and there is less questioning of the parents' view. The mother is in a bad mood and she screams, and the only child thinks: 'It's my fault. She's angry because I'm bad.' A child with siblings can check out what's going on. 'Oh, Mom's in a bad mood again.' That's something that a brother or sister can say, and it's a reality check. Children with siblings don't experience themselves as being the source of the problem as much as only children. . . . If you're constantly told that you're fat, you begin to buy into it, especially if you have no brothers and sisters to say 'I don't think you're fat!' There's no counterview to cause you to question mother's view."

The mother's—or father's—view can be that the only child is extremely good. Not infrequently this happens, and the child can be set up for years of narcissism, frustration and disappointment. But in the only children who come to Forrest for help with eating disorders, the view is just the opposite: They are seen as overly bad. Their self-esteem suffers because of constant criticism from parents who demand perfection and who, when they don't get it, become even more harsh and critical.

Without siblings to absorb some of the criticism and to offer support and another view of reality, the only child can begin to feel that the only way to survive is to do whatever is necessary to get the approval of parents who hold the symbolic power of life and death. It becomes a way a life, even when an only child is not a child anymore, but a thirty-six-year-old woman on her way to the movies.

Theresa Forrest talked about what happened in therapy with Louise. "The problem developed in the relationship with her mother, and I wanted to offer her another relationship in which this could be corrected—a new kind of relationship with a lack of attack and humiliation. She was allowed to experience the absence of threat and the presence of feelings. I encouraged her to have feelings, to try to understand and piece together her present feelings, without any wish to blame her parents for what happened."

Did the therapist in effect become a surrogate mother? No, not exactly. "What therapy did was provide a container, safe and natural, to experience feelings, to promote independence. It was a freeing from the past. She had a fixation to her mother, and bulimia could be seen as a fixation to food, one step removed from the mother. My job was to free her of the fixation . . . She had an addictive, compulsive personality. The compulsion came in and took her over, just as her mother came in and took her over. In therapy I helped her to build self-esteem and confidence to replace her preoccupation with food and weight."

Louise hasn't binged or vomited for more than three years, but she remains in therapy with Forrest to work through some of the issues that seemed to be tied directly to her treatment—or mis-treatment—as an only child. She is learning to appreciate herself, to express herself, to accept herself for what she is rather than condemn herself for what she is not.

It's a story that, at long last, seems to be heading toward a happy ending. When her mother died a few years ago, Louise felt not sadness but a sense of relief. "It's over. I started to come into my own way of thinking."

The High Cost of Unreality

Louise's story certainly is not typical of what happens to only children. I've told her story to make a point: The only child can be the burning focal point of parents' attention and, because of that, can feel compelled in many ways to carry out the wishes and fulfill the dreams of the parents. If the expectations are unrealistic and unrelenting, the only child is at increased risk of developing all sorts of defense mechanisms, most of which are ultimately damaging. What the limited research on this shows is that only children are overrepresented among alcoholics, substance abusers and the obese. These are compulsive behaviors, pitiful attempts to cope with the tension and stress that can stem from demands by parents that their only children be perfect, or at the very least better than everybody else's children.

Psychologist Carol Gantman is aware, from her clients over the years, that the only child is at increased risk of developing anxiety disorders that can be manifested in compulsive behaviors. For the most part the anxiety is tied, in her words, to "feeling very responsible for fulfilling the dreams" that the parents, in one way or another, have invested in the child. There often is an exaggerated need to perform to please the parents. You can see this as early as age three. The child is told to stand up in front of the parents' friends and count from one to ten and then backward from ten to one. We all like to see our children do what they can do, but when the emphasis is on performance rather than 'I love you for who you are,' then you're building trouble. The odds are much greater of this happening with an only child." Why? Because there's no-body else in whom the parents can make an investment.

Not surprisingly, Gantman has found a disproportionate number of anorexics among only children. Mostly these are females whose idea of perfection is to be as slender as possible—even to the point of starvation. For males, because the culture doesn't put the same emphasis on their physical appearance, the reaction to pressure to be perfect can be out-of-control involvement in sports. "A lot of eating disorders are disguised as obsessive activities, marathon running, obsessive exercise, obsessive practice. There's a fine line between healthy involvement in activities and involvement that becomes obsessive and that can be self-destructive."

Yes, a Fine Line

What's the difference between healthy involvement that can enhance us—a positive habit—and obsessive-compulsive behavior that can drag us down? If we can get a handle on that, maybe we can chart a more enlightened course. But sometimes things get terribly fuzzy.

A while back some new exercise equipment was installed in the gymnasium of the condominium where I live, and, because I've followed a vigorous exercise program for years, I was eager to explore new possibilities. First I did the weighted leg lifts, then I rowed and finally I lifted on the hydraulic machine. "Oh, boy," I remarked to a fellow nearby with a glee that was startling even to me. "Now I have something else to be compulsive about."

He said that he sometimes wondered about his passion for exercise, too. "I was at the theater last night, and all through the play I was thinking about getting home and doing my sit-ups. Do you think that's crazy?"

I chose not to deal with the question by remarking "It depends on whether the play was any good." But it did cause me to wonder anew about what's healthy and what's not.

I asked psychiatrist Daniel Lieberman, onetime commissioner of mental health in California, and he said that good habits and compulsive activities are separated only by a matter of degree. In other words, compulsion might be described in part as a good habit gone crazy.

"You take somebody with a compulsive personality, somebody who's clean, neat, always on time, whose life is well-organized, somebody whose exercise program is well established. I don't consider that compulsive in a pathological way. It's a style of living. When you're compelled to do something that is disabling—like excessive drinking—that to me is compulsive. If something bothers you to the point that it interferes with your life, that is compulsive. If you exercise even if your wife is having a baby at that moment, that's compulsive." If the behavior seems to have a life of its own, if it's out of control, that is compulsive.

What triggers compulsive behavior is not fully understood, even by Temple University psychologist Edna Foa, who is one of the nation's leading researchers in this area. Almost forty percent of the people she has treated in the university clinic have been only children and first-born children, who share many of the same characteristics. The personality profile of the obsessive-compulsive person is meticulous, orderly, perfectionistic, "more sensitive to criticism of self," said Foa. Those with this profile are more prone to develop obsessive disorders if they are controlled by parents who are overprotective, punishing or demanding. One of the questions with which researchers are grappling is whether the same mechanism underlies all obsessive disorders, said Foa. "You have people who take twenty-five showers a day and people who check a hundred times to see if the door is locked or if the stove is turned off. And you have people who are compulsive about gambling, eating, smoking. People can derive joy from gambling, eating and smoking, but I don't know anybody who enjoys washing or checking. They're doing something they don't like to do," yet they continue—and nobody knows why.

Psychiatrist Jean Spaulding of Duke University treats many young women with anorexia, and the development of the disorder not infrequently stems from pressure to be perfect, she said. "Their response to the pressure is to try to gain control . . . and their controlling what they eat or don't eat sometimes is an attempt to make themselves perfect." By extension, they are attempting to make the world perfect, too.

Denial: Maybe the Worst Disorder of All

Denial is a defense mechanism that we've all used, and at times it can be helpful. The person who denies that it's impossible for him to do something often goes out and does it, while another person hangs back. But denial can be terribly damaging. Just ask any alcoholic who, at the point of death, denied that he had a problem. What I want to share now is a story that I haven't talked about much because I'm not proud of it. It's a story that is especially relevant to only children, many of whom, like me, hold the supreme belief that they are in control of their lives, masters of their fate, that by sheer force of will they can alter the natural course of events. It sounds silly, but because we've been told for so long that we are so special, that we can do anything and everything, we've come to believe it.

Years ago, if you had asked me to sketch my philosophical approach to life, I would have said something like "You only have problems if you think you have problems." An extension of that was my attitude toward illness: "You're only sick if you think you're sick." I felt that I had such a strong barrier against physical illness that it approached total immunity. My position was that I was calling the shots, that no illness was going to slow me down, let alone put me to bed, and that if I didn't offer illness the upper hand by acknowledging it and surrendering to it, I could go forever on my merry, healthy way.

The strange thing was that this seemed to work for many years. Yes, I had days when I didn't feel up to snuff, when I'd rather have rolled over and gone back to sleep, but I kept going, if not at full speed at least fast enough so that nobody except those who knew me best could tell any difference. On the days when I felt sluggish, I pushed myself hardest and turned out some of my best work. For more than a decade, from my thirties into my forties, the only office time I missed was when I slipped on the ice and suffered a fractured elbow. I was out of action two whole days because of that.

Although the drumbeat was mine alone, I sometimes had trouble understanding why others didn't march to it, too. That's a mind-set that I've found to be peculiar to only children. "If it works for me, it will work for you, too." Back when I was a

60

newspaper editor, I tended to be scornful of people who called in sick, who surely must have thought that I was crazy when I said things like "Come on in and you'll feel better." Even after I left the editorship in North Carolina and started writing my column in Philadelphia, I was annoyed by people who limped into the office, sneezed a few times and went home. They were participating in the victory of illness over themselves, I felt, and if they just buckled down, ignored it and worked harder, they'd be as good as new in no time at all. Just look at me—I was proof positive that mind over body really paid off.

To some extent I still believe this, even now—that there is virtue in not giving in too quickly to illness. That's another thing I've found to be peculiar to only children: We don't surrender easily. But I've also found out, the hard way, that it's possible to ride a good horse right off the edge of a cliff by not paying attention to where you're going.

Some years ago I began to feel increasingly tired and weak, which was unusual for me, since my energy level normally is quite high. My response was not to find out what was going on but to deny that anything was wrong—deny it to the point at which I almost had ceased to function. When I finally went to the doctor, it was not because I was feeling awful but because it was time for my annual physical examination. What the doctor found, when the laboratory analyzed my blood, was that my thyroid activity virtually had died—a condition induced by another doctor who unwisely had prescribed iodine as part of the treatment for my allergies.

"How much longer could I have gone on like this?" I asked my doctor. Well, he said, that was hard to say, "but there would have come a morning, not too far off, when you wouldn't have had the strength to get up. Probably sometime after that, you would have died." I waited for him to smile, but he never did. He prescribed a thyroid supplement, and in a few weeks I was back at full speed.

Wouldn't you think that an adult—even a walk-on-water only child—would learn something from that? I wish that I could tell you that I did, but I didn't. A few years later I slipped right back into my old denials, my old unwillingness to come to grips with the reality that I didn't feel well, despite growing awareness that something bad might be happening to me.

It began sometime before Christmas when I had to rely more heavily on steroids to quell symptoms of my late-onset asthma. Did I telephone my doctor and say "Hey, I need help"? No, I waited until my next regularly scheduled appointment in two months, and by then I regularly was running a low-grade fever and feeling fatigued and drained, no matter if I slept ten or even twelve hours, which I was doing with increasing frequency.

My denial of reality was awesome. As if to prove to myself that I really wasn't feeling too terrible, I took the car to the river and washed and polished it, although my temperature, by the time I got home, was 102. "I'll be okay tomorrow," I told my wife when she fussed at me. But I wasn't okay tomorrow or the day after. Fortunately I was saved from myself by the long-scheduled appointment with my doctor, who knew my craziness well enough not to be hesitant about chewing me out.

"What's the matter with you? Why didn't you call? Why didn't you come to see me earlier?"

He immediately hospitalized me as an emergency patient. I was there for eight days—the fever at one time bordered on 105—and I was treated for acute inflammation of the air ducts in the upper right lung, a condition brought on by my body's unpredictable response to nonspecific allergens.

As I lay in my hospital room and studied the ceiling, I also studied my behavior—what it had done to me in the past, what it was doing to me at that very moment, what it surely would do to me again if I didn't change.

So I decided to change my bad habit of denial by paying attention to my doctor, who told me: "Your body talks to you, and you need to listen." These days I'm listening, and if it's not too late, I want to apologize to the people at whom I smirked when they called in sick.

Yes, the good news is that we can change. It works not only for compulsive behaviors but for other bad habits also.

Speaking of Bad Habits, Such as Work

For some only children, work becomes a compulsion, as they strive for perfection, to make their parents proud of them, to show the world just how great they really are, to try to live up to their ideal self-image—no matter how unrealistic it may be. The whole subject of workaholism and the only child will be explored more fully in the next chapter, but it's appropriate to talk about it briefly here in the context of compulsive behavior. It's something in which I have more personal experience than I wish I had, because for many years I worked twelve or fourteen hours a day, not because I enjoyed it especially but because I couldn't help it. I was out of control.

Nobody I know has ever tried to count the number of only children among glassy-eyed workaholics, but the number surely must be substantial. As only children, we are geared to achievement and if we aren't achieving "enough," however much that is, then the answer obviously is to work harder and longer. It's damaging, but many of us don't realize that for a long time—until after our children become strangers to us, our marriages break, our health pales. Achievement is chased not because it represents a step in the process of life but because it's an end in itself. When achievement is sought for the sake of achievement, we lose perspective and control of our lives.

What happens? Why do we go crazy? Psychiatrist Erwin Smarr said that commitment to work is healthy when it's based on a person's desire to take care of himself and his family. But it becomes unhealthy when it's grounded in neurotic muck, and it's here that the workaholic always is found. Some men are driven to work hard out of their need to compete with other males, including authority figures. "They wish to be like the authority figures, and also they have the drive to surpass them and to be strong enough to get out from under their domination. And so work becomes a pathway to achievement of freedom through getting enough money and position to get out from under and to become one's own boss." But the hook is that no amount of success is enough for some people, especially only children, who are driven by their competitiveness and parental expectation to be perfect. So their workaholism continues regardless of how much success they achieve. Said Smarr: "Often they derive more satisfaction from pursuing their drive to be perfect than from other activities and relationships."

While he and others tend to talk about workaholism primarily as a male affliction, it really binds up women, too. As more women are motivated by the same drives as men to achieve more and to compete for status, money and power, they can become as workaholic as men and show the same kinds of stress effects of compulsiveness as men.

Psychologist Marilyn Machlowitz agrees with that. In 1980, after five years of research and interviews, including one with me, she wrote the groundbreaking book *Workaholics: Living with Them, Working with Them.* She told me that when she first started, the term "workaholic" mostly was applied to men, but it's different these days because so many women in the corporate world feel that they must surpass men in all areas to be considered as good as men. Women have the same insecurities as men, and the only children among them are driven by the same needs to achieve.

In the Beginning . . .

The seeds that eventually sprout into compulsive achievement can be planted early in the life of an only child by parents who want the child to have "a better life."

Leon Katz, a Philadelphia judge who is the son of Jewish immigrants from Russia, told me a story that, while more extreme than most, carries a familiar theme: "I can remember when I was three or four years old, and my mother would hold me on her lap and rock me and sing to me with words that she made up as she went along. The words indicated clearly that when I grew up I would be a doctor or a lawyer, have a nice car and a big house. That was the indoctrination I got. There was nothing implicit about it. She sent me direct messages that I was expected to be a big success."

A businesswoman told me that her mother gave her direct messages, too: "The first time I can remember, I was just a little girl, and I came into the kitchen one morning and there was Mama on her hands and knees, scrubbing the floor, and she looked so tired. She stopped working for a minute, asked me to come closer and, when I did, she hugged me so hard that I thought I was going to break. She was crying. I remember that so well. It was the first time I ever saw her cry. She said 'This is what happens to a woman

64

who doesn't get an education. Don't let this happen to you.' I didn't exactly know what she meant, but in the years after that she repeated the message in ways that made it quite understandable. That's why I made up my mind that I was going to be somebody special."

Yes, special. Parents can act out that expectation in many ways. One common way is called "hothousing," and it's the practice of parents' pushing their young children to achieve too much too soon, confronting them with premature challenges. Some children respond and zoom right past their peers, much to the delight of their parents, but many others become discouraged and defeated. If you studied children who are hothoused, you would find that only children are overrepresented among them—not because they necessarily have greater potential but because their parents have higher expectations.

Psychologist Judith Coche, herself an only child who is the mother of an only child, said that most parents "who are well-meaning have certain value systems, and their system, whatever it is, determines the hothousing, not the number of children. But many with the hothousing value system wouldn't think of having three or four or five children. It's a value system that holds that achievement is more important than learning to play, that competition is more important than cooperation, that more is better. If you put all your eggs in one basket, you want the basket to be special," and this is the only child who typically is hothoused.

Coche said that parents should aim to help the child maximize achievement, which is completely unlike hothousing, although some parents seem not to understand the difference. Maximizing achievement involves the concept of readiness, when a child is ready to learn something. Parents and teachers have in their own best interest and in the child's best interest an obligation to help the child move to the next level of complexity in whatever activity is involved. Hothousing, trying to create the so-called "super-baby," is quite different. In Coche's view this does not maximize achievement. To the contrary, it frustrates achievement because the child's readiness is not taken into account by the parents, who are asking the child to advance at a rate that they impose, not one that is necessarily appropriate for the child.

A story from Coche's experience with her own daughter: "The best stimulation to teach a child a foreign language is to take the child to the country in which the language is spoken. We were tempted to try to teach our daughter German before she was ready. [Coche's husband, psychologist Erich Coche, is from Germany.] We took her to Germany when she was six, but she wasn't ready, and she didn't learn." But a year later, she told her parents that she was ready, "and we put her in an environment that made it impossible for her not to learn."

What motivates parents who hothouse their child? One reason can be that they are trying to live vicariously through their child's accomplishment, said Coche. Another reason can be that parents who are themselves hothoused achievers view overprogrammed activity as "a kind of preferable substitute for more traditional kinds of instructional daycare, babysitting or play groups. The idea is that the child has to be somewhere while the parents are away, and it might as well be in a situation in which the child can put the time to good use." Translation: A child shouldn't "waste" time playing. This is one reason why some only children, not without bitterness, have remarked to me and to therapists that they felt as if they never had a childhood. They were asked to grow up before their time.

The result of this tends not to be good for anybody. The child doesn't learn and the parents are frustrated and critical. This can set the stage for a lifetime of struggling, of the child's attempting to be good enough to please the parents, of trying to make up to the parents for falling short, of turning to self-destructive, compulsive behaviors to try to dull the pain.

Said therapist Theresa Forrest: "If the unreasonable or impossible is expected of you and if you fall short and then the fault-finding starts, you're in trouble . . . and you try to escape any way you can."

Compulsive behavior isn't always the result, but unhappiness surely is.

4

Hi Ho, Hi Ho,
It's Off to Work We Go . . . and Go

It was in the early 1970s, and I was sitting in my office as executive editor of *The Charlotte News* in North Carolina. It wasn't a good day for me because of what had happened the night before. As usual, I had come home late, after a work day that had spanned almost thirteen hours, and my older son Jay, who then was fifteen, had stuck it to me with uncharacteristic sarcasm.

"Anybody can be a biological father," he said, "and that's about all you are. If you were a *real* father, you wouldn't be the way you are."

I knew what was coming, and, maybe because I felt guilty, I opened the door and invited it in. "Why don't you tell me, Jay, about the way I am?"

"All you do is work. Doesn't anything else matter to you? Aren't we important to you? What kinds of memories are we going to have when we grow up—with an absentee father?"

I was nailed to the cross, and I knew it, but I wasn't about to acknowledge it, guilty or not.

"Look, Jay, I work hard so we can have a better life. I'm doing it for you as much as for me." It was a crimson-face lie, and Jay treated it that way.

"Don't do me any favors!"

I didn't sleep well that night, because Jay's accusation haunted me. Why *did* I work so long and so hard? What was the payoff?

67

Was I exercising free will when I spent so much time at the newspaper? Or was I driven by some force that was beyond my control, that had a life of its own?

Oh, well, I had to get on with the day's business, and for me that began before 7:00 A.M., with the early edition of the afternoon newspaper, and then the news conference, and then there was the mail to wade through and then . . .

Grant was my second-born son, fourteen at the time and editor of his junior high school newspaper. This was the morning that he was to bring his journalism class on a tour of our building, and it was an important time for him because for this event he was the leader of the class, not the teacher, who had delegated command for the moment to the kid who had connections with the executive editor.

I looked through the glass wall of my office out into the newsroom, and I saw the first of the students meandering in, looking in awe at the reporters sitting at their terminals and punching in their stories, at the editors who screamed incessantly for speed and brevity. Then there was Grant, taller than the others, who moved to the head of the pack and directed everybody back toward my office. I waved, and he smiled and waved back. He poked his head through the door and greeted me with unrestrained enthusiasm: "Hi, Dad!"

A student who came about up to Grant's shoulders seemed unduly impressed by me and my office. "Gosh, Grant, is that really your father? What does he do?" Grant's smile disappeared, and his enthusiasm was replaced by what sounded like resignation. "What does he do? Mostly he works."

Yes, for many years that's mostly what I did, and my frantic pace continued until I finally was jolted by a broken marriage and the realization that I had two sons who were growing up without my really knowing them. My salvation came when I was able to separate who I am as a person from what I do for a living. That sounds simple enough, but it was difficult for me, and it is difficult for many only children, I think, because we are so achievement-oriented, so committed to success that we are in danger of becoming what we do for a living. There's another element to our workaholism, too, one that seldom is discussed, and it is this: More than children with siblings, we view our parents as our primary source of love, nurturing and nourishment, and, when the time comes to separate from them, we tend to look for somebody or something to which we can transfer our need to be special and worthy of praise. Robert Schwartz, who runs a school for entrepreneurs at his conference center in Tarrytown, New York, once described it to me this way: "We go around like a lightbulb looking for a socket to screw into to get some juice." For many of us, especially the men, this socket is our employment. In effect, we adopt the corporation as surrogate parents, and in return for the juice we pledge our last drop of dedication. The wonder is not that so many of us become workaholics but that even a few of us manage to escape.

So it's hi ho . . . and off to work we go. The solution to every problem is to work harder, and when that doesn't get the hoped-for result, we assume the flaw is that we didn't work quite hard enough. It's a blueprint for disaster, and I've talked to enough only children over the years to believe that disaster is the destination at which many of us eventually arrive, whether it's broken health, alcoholism, drug abuse, obesity, divorce, poverty in personal relationships or the absence of any lasting peace of mind.

How did I become a workaholic? In large measure I got it from my father, but not in the way you might think. Let me tell you a story.

The Early Years That Molded the Man

I was the keynote speaker at a day-long seminar on "You and Your Father," which was billed as an exploration of how you and your life have been shaped by your father's influence. It was an unusually moving event because of my only-child closeness to my father. It prompted me to retrieve my earliest memories of my relationship with him, to dissect that relationship and weigh its impact on my life as an adult. It's a challenging, intriguing exercise, and I suggest you try it sometime. What I found was not new to me, but it was brought more sharply into focus, and I had the sense that Dad and I were sitting on the floor, as we so often did when I came home to visit, talking the night away about our yesterdays and how they colored our todays and our tomorrows.

Dad had been wiped out financially and devastated emotionally by the Great Depression, which robbed him not only of his job and the house in which I was born but of virtually everything else as well—except his will to survive. In the two years after I was born, he worked a total of four months and, as his meager savings dwindled to a few hundred dollars, he tightened his belt notch after notch and grimly plowed on.

We survived, better than many families, Dad always said, because we didn't have as far to fall in our standard of living as many families. We were relatively poor before the Depression, too, and the only difference now was that there was nothing relative about it: We were *very* poor.

"It taught me that a man can get along if he makes up his mind," Dad said. "I guess that's what in later years always made me sort of a miser. At least I always thought you felt that I was awfully tight with the money when you were growing up. That's why. I got that way back then when I learned not to spend a penny I didn't have to spend."

As an adolescent, I often clashed with Dad over money and screeched at him more times than I like to recall: "What's money for if it's not to spend?" To his credit Dad never screeched back. Instead, he was prone to respond with a question: "If you throw it away on everything, what are you going to do when there's something you need, or really want?" Even as an adolescent, I could understand that, and to some extent it became a cornerstone of what fiscal philosophy I possess today. While I couldn't be described as tightfisted with money, I think that I am reasonably prudent, and before even semi-major purchases I ask myself such questions as "Do I need this? Does buying this constitute being nice to myself or being self-indulgent? What would happen if I didn't buy this?" Dad's philosophy is there, watered down to be sure, but nonetheless it's a part of me, and I like it.

Dad's other major influence on me is one that I don't like. He never consciously pushed it on me, but it happened, a product of the hard times in which we lived. Dad was scarred forever by the Depression, which left him with a craving for security that outweighed everything else, including work that was satisfying. Because of what had happened to him, he was leached of his desire to take risks, to venture into the darkness of uncertainty with the expectation that what he found would be better than what he had left. Some of his bosses capitalized on this and treated him shabbily, because they knew that he would neither fight back nor quit.

The legacy that Dad unknowingly left me in this area was ugly: Don't ever get in a position where anybody can exploit you; climb, climb the hill of success so that if there's any exploiting, it's done to somebody else. For me this translated into a crazy kind of workaholism that made my sons seem like strangers to me and that at one point jeopardized my health and my inclination to look at the world through anybody's porthole except mine. It took me many years and many hard knocks to unravel all of that, but in the process I found out who I was and emerged with a value system that was far less rigid and much more reality-based.

What was my legacy to my sons, who through my work-crazed years must have wondered many times if the merry-go-round was ever going to stop spinning? The double message I gave them was baffling: Career success is all that matters, but career success doesn't bring happiness. Out of that muck, though, they distilled philosophies that should take them on ulcer-free journeys through life: Don't take work as a life-or-death matter; work is only one of many important things and should not be pursued to the exclusion of other things that are important, too—such as relationships and good times.

Once when Grant was visiting in Philadelphia, he marveled at what he viewed as my relaxed, unstructured life as a writer, and I asked if he would like a similar job someday. His response—"No, because I know what you had to do to get here"—was an unveiled reference to my years in the trenches as an editor, when he and Jay were growing up and when, we all agreed later, I hollered too much and enjoyed life too little. I wish I could have been a more positive model in influencing my sons, that they could have become something of what I was rather than much of what I was not. But that's all part of fathering, isn't it? The good news is that, as adults, they have their careers in perspective. They are not—and I think they never will be—workaholics.

The Light Stays On

Ned Klumph is a career consultant in Cherry Hill, New Jersey, and, unlike many people in his line of work, he actually had a successful career before he became a consultant. He once was chief executive officer of a Japanese corporation and before that he was an executive for a number of Fortune 500 companies. He remembers vividly what it was like when he was called in by his boss many years ago and given his first big promotion:

"He said: 'Klumph, we like what you're doing. Everybody around here says that the light never goes out in your office.'"

That, said Klumph, was his first indication that the wonderful world of big business put heavy emphasis on the length of the workday as a measurement of an up-and-coming executive's potential. It seemed to matter less what Klumph accomplished than how long it took him to accomplish it, and the rule seemed to be the longer the better. It was a lesson that Klumph, in his ladder-climbing days, never forgot. In the years that followed, he made certain that the light never went out in his office because he stayed there, often until after midnight, even if he had nothing to do. After all, they were watching. But there was no way they could know that he was playing solitaire.

Over the years I've probably written more columns about workaholism than about anything else, about how single-minded commitment to career can wreck not only your life apart from work but eventually your work, too, because a candle, burned for so long at both ends, flickers and dies. It's a subject that readers around the country respond to with passion . . . and sometimes with what seems like desperation.

There was a man, twenty-nine, with a six-month-old son: "I now begin my life as a father, and already I begin to understand what a tremendous responsibility it is to be a father. I must now shape in whatever way fortune dictates the life of my son . . . As an aspiring photojournalist, I have been somewhat dismayed and even slightly discouraged by your account of your years in the trenches and the unfortunate disposition of your marriage. It's obvious that to succeed in a career such as yours the involvement and commitment must be extraordinary or at least competitive with others in the same field. This characteristic of the journalistic vocation seems to invite the kind of workaholism that you have described. I already have had minor skirmishes with my wife over my priorities in accepting assignments that take me away from home and that demand a portion of the attention that she feels belongs to her. I am seriously dedicated to my work and must compete with a group of talented, ambitious and equally dedicated colleagues who, in my experience, seem almost fanatical in their desire to succeed. . . .

"Is it possible to succeed in this kind of career these days and not have it resolve itself only through dissolved marriage or failing health? Surely, there is a middle ground between these two extremes. In light of these considerations, your comments about your preoccupation with your work during your sons' growing-up years really hit home. The scary thing is I'm not really sure that I won't do the same thing with my only child. . . . Is it possible to make it in a career and not destroy everything else that's important?"

Edward H. Kuljian is president of his own consulting firm in Philadelphia, and until it was sold a decade ago, he was chief executive officer of Kuljian Corporation, a family-owned business that designed and built power plants and industrial projects around the world.

It's a fact, said Kuljian, that business, for the most part, still demands the last drop of blood from those on the way up, despite all the talk that's going around about the importance of a balanced life. It's not uncommon, he said, for a chief executive officer to call a Sunday afternoon meeting, to tell you to forget your weekend and come to the meeting. "If you analyze what caused the urgency, you can't find anything. But if you say that, no, you can't come to the meeting because it's your daughter's birthday, then your loyalty is judged to be misplaced."

In many ways climbing the corporate ladder means that you've sold yourself into a corporate bondage that pays extremely well. "A boss says that he'll pay you twice what you're now making if you come to work for him, but the caveat is 'Now that I own you body and soul, I don't want any nonsense when I call you at two in the morning. I don't want to hear about your going on vacation or planning a free weekend.' " No matter what anybody says, corporations still tend to look for the kind of "dedication" that is reflected in long hours. "The consequences usually are horribly damaging to any family relationship."

Ned Klumph recalled a man in his twenties who was telling him that he was going to climb the corporate ladder right to the top and that no price was too high for the success that was going to be his. "I told him to come back when he was forty and tell me that, but he didn't understand what I meant. It's something that you can't tell people. They have to go through it themselves to see how crazy it is."

Is it possible to make it big without shortchanging everything else in life? Probably not in the corporate world, Klumph thought, and that's why some people who spend much of a lifetime married to their career, when they finally figure it out, leave newspaper editorships and Fortune 500 executive suites.

What do I think? I think that in launching any career a high price must be paid in terms of investment of time and energy. The trap into which so many of us fall is that we fail to recognize when we've reached the point at which this high price no longer is essential to our success. So we continue to work and work, kidding ourselves into thinking we are working for "the family." When we look around one day and the family isn't there anymore, we wonder what happened.

Something to Think About

Psychologist Julian Slowinski opened the letter from a longtime friend and colleague with whom he was collaborating on yet another article that would be published in yet another professional journal. The colleague said that it was a lot of work, a whole lot of work. Wistfully, it seemed, he asked three questions: Why are we doing it? How much is enough? What does it all mean?

Slowinski thought about the time that the dreaded telephone call had come: "Julian, your father is dying. Please get here as quickly as you can." In the car, grieving as he drove, Slowinski found that a verse from Psalms kept running through his mind:

"Fear of the Lord is the beginning of wisdom." The application of that verse to everyday life was obvious to him. "You need a reference for things. You need to learn to slow down and put things in proper perspective . . . Over the long haul, what's really important—to sign that big deal or to experience life more fully?" What is really important, he concluded, is balance, that often difficult-to-achieve blend of work and play. With all his heart he believed it, and he would work to help himself and others reach it.

Slowinski, who is the father of an only child, regularly witnesses in his psychological practice the residue of lives that are out of control, without balance, wrecked by blind allegiance to career success at any price.

"People get into the achievement-oriented rat race, and they can't get out. The stress often is incredible because people have no time for anything but work. . . . I see college kids who are neurotic about getting straight A's so they can be admitted to medical school. They forego all pleasures in life to try to get straight A's. . . . I see kids come out of the Wharton School and get onto Wall Street and in a couple of years they're chewed up and spit out and burned out."

Slowinski continued: "We get in the way of our own happiness because we put our whole ego into the job. . . . This business of 'I am a psychologist, you are a journalist' bothers me. There's a lot more to a person than that, but it takes some reflection often for us to realize it." And it often takes some commitment for us to act on it. "We need to take time to have a concept of ourselves and to understand what we see as really important. On the death-bed, we always wish we had done this or that. The trick is to do it while we're alive."

Success: What Is It?

It's unfortunate, and it doesn't make any sense, but society adopts workaholics as role models and encourages its young people to emulate them. This is damaging, the perception that unless you work yourself to a frazzle, forsake all recreation and family life, you're somehow being counterproductive to your own success. We need to use as role models those who show the value of balance in life, who unquestionably work hard but who admit to enjoying balanced lives. A problem with our society is that anybody who suggests contentment with what he has achieved, who doesn't constantly push for more, is regarded as a loser. He's copping out. People say, "Well, he's making ends meet, but who would want to be like him?" The role-model phenomenon bothers me and many people with whom I talk. If you're making big dollars, if you achieve a huge takeover or get to the top spot, then you are a "success." Even if the rest of your life is a shambles.

I have a question that I often pose for those before whom I am invited to speak: "What is your definition of success?" What I find is that almost nobody can answer the question because almost nobody has thought about it seriously. We've accepted society's historical definition—more is better—and we're very much like the fellow who was pictured on the cover of *Esquire* magazine's "success" issue a few years ago. We're hanging onto the back of a speeding commuter train and we look as if we know where we're going, but in truth we're simply following the rails, going wherever the train takes us, and pretending, whether it's true or not, that it's our destination of choice.

Some success we can measure. When Jonas Salk finds a cure for polio, that's success. When we send a man to the moon, that's success. But it begins to get questionable when we try to measure success in a career. Take somebody who's a corporate chief executive officer with a high six-figure income. Is he automatically a success? Is John DeLorean a success? Are you a success if you drink too much, if you're always tired, if your spouse won't talk to you, if your child is angry with you, if you have a heart attack, if you're alone at fifty, if your Maalox consumption has tripled, if the job is all you've got in the whole world? Is that success?

I ask people to define success in terms of what their daily lives would be like. Where would they work? What hours would they work? What would they do? How would they dress? What would happen after work? Then I suggest that they ask their spouse and children to define what success means to them. Is everybody's definition fairly similar? Or is the distance staggering? I have a notion that there's a lot of distance in most families. My suspicion is that the husband would say: "I'd consider myself a success if I made $175,000 and was senior vice-president with a corner office on a high floor." The wife would probably say: "I'd think we were successful if we spent more time together as a family." The twelve-year-old boy says: "I'd think we were successful if somebody came to watch me play Little League once in a while."

We need to ask this critical question—for ourselves, for those we purport to love.

The Search for Life's Meaning

Harold Kushner is rabbi of Temple Israel in Natick, Massachusetts, near Boston, and a successful author who is much in demand as a speaker. He told me that in the work world there surely is a time to throttle back and begin to sniff the roses. But when?

"It was Carl Jung who said that the agenda of life's morning is the agenda of achievement and that the agenda of life's afternoon has to be different. You spend the first part of life finding out how good you are, how far you can go, but then . . . I was speaking to a group in Orange County, California, about how power corrupts, isolates, distorts relationships, encourages us to see people as things to be used. The first question from the audience was 'How can I teach my college-age kid to be less competitive?' My answer was 'You can't, and you shouldn't.' Nothing would happen in the world if young people didn't try hard to succeed. But you've got to get to the point where you say 'I got it.' Either the dream's true or it's not true. If it's not true, you've got to change dreams . . . If Act One of life is goal-oriented—'How far can I go?'—then Act Two is 'How can I put it all together and achieve something permanent?' The answer to that has got to involve your connecting with people."

Kushner said that it's not possible and probably not wise anyway to try to teach this lesson to young people because it's a lesson that can be learned only by traveling the road of hard experience. "A reporter asked me what I know now that I wish I'd known at twenty-five. I said 'Nothing.' You've got to go through it and learn from your mistakes. To young people I would say 'Don't change, but realize it's a phase you're going through.' Take a man of thirty who shelves his family while he succeeds in business. I wouldn't tell him to stop. But I would ask him to realize that there is a time to stop and a price to be paid while he's ignoring his family. I wish that I had been less self-righteous when I was thirty and ignoring my family because I wanted to be the best rabbi in America. I wish I had thought of it as a need that I had then, rather than telling people to get off my back."

Kushner said that the people who mellow out and cut themselves loose from the chains of workaholism are those who listen to themselves, to what their minds and bodies are saying, to what those who matter are telling them. Those who refuse to change don't listen. Instead they deny and suppress.

"You feel blah when you wake up. It's easy to say 'I had too much to eat . . . Not enough exercise . . . It's my biorhythm.' They don't admit that life is blah. The worst pain is the pain we don't know we're suffering. We believe that life is supposed to be smog, traffic jams and high prices. . . . My father was in Lithuania in World War I, and he talked about how people went out in the morning and asked who died last night. . . . People have an ache at the center of their being and no way of knowing it's not supposed to feel like that."

Some people are pushed into recognition of the pain by trauma—illness, divorce or problems with their children. But others don't need trauma. They come to midlife and look at time differently. They know that life is finite, that they're not going to live forever.

"My father's death at eighty-four was not trauma," said Kushner. "Four years before, he stopped being the man he had been. But his death was a statement of mortality—his and mine. I look in the mirror today and realize how much I resemble my father at fifty. It's not trauma, but it puts me in touch with time. It teaches me to look at time differently. If you do that, a lot of questions appear on the agenda."

I asked Kushner what he would say to young, bright-eyed career people who are on the fast elevator to the top floor. "I would ask them to think of the happiest people they know. They're probably not the people who buy the happiness books and take happiness courses. They're probably not the most famous, the most affluent. The happiest people probably work at being good, honest, reliable neighbors and friends. If the goal of life is to be happy, we can learn a lesson from these people. . . . Young businesspeople need to have their eyes on the top rung. But they should know that they will have to pay a price for this and that if all they learn how to do well is to be a good manager of whatever, life will be distorted for them. At some point, as Carl Jung said, we have to go back and fill in the spaces we left blank earlier in life."

Seth Isaiah Rubin is an analytical psychologist who trained at the Jung Institute in Zurich, Switzerland, where his thesis dealt with midlife transition. In his private practice he so often encounters only children in middle age who, no matter how hard they have worked and how much they have succeeded, are gripped by the nagging sense that there has to be something more to life than all of this.

"To get to where you are, you have to exclude parts of your personality. You get to the point where you're out of balance, and this often is manifested as a sense of frustration. You've achieved your goals, but you're not particularly satisfied with what you've got. You thought that when you got there, everything would be great. But it's not great. It's a real letdown, almost as if life has cheated you. To excel, you have to become one-sided, and eventually this catches up with you."

When Things Go Sour . . .

To psychiatrist Peter Brill, the workaholic's life is "like a spring-loaded device" that can go haywire, fall apart or blow up. It gets off track and tends to get worse. Every step aimed at correction seems to make things worse.

Brill was the psychiatrist in a classic case that involved not one workaholic but two—husband and wife—and Brill saw what it's like when a spring-loaded device detonates. Here's the story:

Both were hard workers, absorbed totally in their careers from the very beginning of their marriage. The husband was a lawyer; the wife sold computers. Only children themselves, they had no children because they had no time for anything except work. They had the world by the tail, it seemed, until on a ski trip the wife suffered a broken leg. "What happened after that was unbelievable," said Brill. "The wife began to regress. At home alone, she became mildly depressed and more needy. She began to make demands on her husband for nurturing. The husband's response was to get angry. He saw her demands as an abridgment of the marital contract.

"She became even more demanding, and the husband went bananas. This was not the kind of woman he'd married. What was wrong with her?"

And the wife began to wonder what kind of person she had indeed become. When Brill saw them in therapy, they were at the edge of divorce. "I calmed down the husband, filled some of the dependency needs of the wife. That stabilized the situation, but the residual effect on the marriage was tremendous. Her self-confidence was shaken, and she thought that she was a terribly needy, dependent person."

If You Can Find Your Orange Ball . . .

Anybody can become a workaholic. It doesn't happen just to the only child. And anybody can stop being a workaholic, even the only child. But the stopping doesn't happen all by itself. We have to make a decision to change, and then we have to follow through on the decision. But once we're free, it can be glorious. It *is* glorious. Let me tell you another story:

It was the beginning of a long weekend, and I was alone at our beach place, except for my cat, B.G., who makes the transition between the city and the seashore as rapidly and completely as I do. I was tired, and I had gone to bed about eleven o'clock, right in the middle of my favorite radio program of classical music. B.G. was in his usual spot at the foot of the bed, between my ankles. I'm a sound sleeper, and it's rare for me to wake up before daylight, but there I was—suddenly awake at 2:00 A.M. There was no noise, except for the rhythmic crashing of the waves. So what had broken my sleep?

I rolled toward the window, and there it was—the moon, sitting like a giant orange ball where the sky met the sea, spraying a path of shimmering light across the water and right into the bedroom. I lay there in awe, because I'd never seen anything so spectacular. It was as if I could reach out and touch it, that orange ball, which at that instant represented to me everything in life that was beautiful and meaningful, yet fragile and fleeting.

I said aloud to myself: "This is why I woke up. Otherwise I'd have missed it." I reached down and pulled B.G. up onto the pillow and spoke quietly: "Look. This is a magic moment. Aren't we lucky to be here? It's something we'll always remember." B.G. shook loose from my grasp, growled with what sounded like absolute disgust, returned to his place and immediately slipped back into dreamland. "The problem with you, B.G.," I said, "is that you're like some people I know—too wrapped up in other things to recognize what's really important."

I turned back to the window and gazed out for a while longer, until the moon was higher and had changed to its customary silver. The orange ball was gone, but not the magic. Even if B.G. doesn't remember, I always will.

What is life all about? I remember reading some of what Kushner wrote in *When All You've Ever Wanted Isn't Enough:* "When we stop searching for the Great Answer, the Immortal Deed which will give our lives ongoing meaning, and instead concentrate on filling our individual days with moments that gratify us, then we will find the only possible answer to the question: What is life about? It is not about writing great books, amassing great wealth, achieving great power. It is about loving and being loved. It is about enjoying your food and sitting in the sun rather than rushing through lunch and hurrying back to the office. It is about savoring the beauty of the moments that don't last, the sunsets, the leaves turning color, the rare moments of true human communication. It is about savoring them rather than missing out on them because we are so busy, and they will not hold still until we get around to them."

Life, I am convinced, is all about taking time to appreciate the orange ball, in whatever shape and at whatever time and place we encounter it. If we don't recognize it when it's there, we have missed a big part of life and, in some way, we have died a little—because we are less than we could have been.

—— 5 ——

Achievement: Ecstasy and Agony

It was a sunny morning in September, opening day of another busy school term at the Medical College of Pennsylvania, and Selma Kramer, professor of child psychiatry, was meeting with first-year students, as she always does, and asking a question she always asks: "How many of you are only children or first-born children?"

There was some foot shuffling and a ripple of conversation. This was, after all, not the kind of question the students had expected.

Kramer, a grandmother and one of the big names worldwide in her field, smiled patiently. "Go ahead, please, and raise your hands, all of you who are only children or first-born."

Reluctantly at first, a few hands went up. Then more and more. Eventually, it seemed that almost every hand in the auditorium was raised. Kramer acknowledged the students with a nod before she spoke: "Thank you. That's about what I expected to see."

The same thing happens every year, Kramer would say later. At first it surprised her, but now she's accustomed to it: About eighty percent of the beginning medical students are only children or first-born. "It's not that the parents' genes dissolve after the first child, but that child gets much more parental time and is primed with higher expectations. You look around at all professional schools, and that's what you'll find, many more first-borns, and, of course, that's what the only child is, first-born."

The only child, more than any other child, tends to get the message early and often that he is special, capable . . . and *expected* to make it big. The up side of this is that only children do tend to be more successful than others in their careers, to achieve above and beyond everybody else. But the down side, in Kramer's view, is that "if they don't achieve and live up to expectations, their parents and their own, they can have terrible self-esteem." Some only children, weary of being inundated with their parents' achievement messages, rebel and don't achieve much of anything. "They dig in their heels and don't do well." Others try with all their might but never quite get the sense of acceptance and approval that they so desperately seek. "When you're told that you've got to achieve, that you're so special, you almost can have feelings of failure no matter what you achieve. If you're a good lawyer but your father wanted you to be a judge, you can feel like a failure. If you don't meet parental expectations for achievement, it's almost inevitable that you'll feel that you weren't good enough. . . . But it's hard for parents to hear it when they're told not to expect too much." What makes it so hard? It's because the only child is seen as so capable . . . and so special.

She was in her first year of medical school when I talked with her, a bright, energetic, curious, warm young woman who seemed marvelously old-fashioned. She wanted to be a family doctor, like her father and grandfather, because she wanted to get to know her patients so that she could give them better medical care. "I'm not going into medicine because I want to make a lot of money. I want to help people."

An only child, she felt secure and well-loved by her busy father, who occasionally took her with him to his office and to the hospital, and by her mother, who was a nurse. "They worked as hard as any two people I ever heard of, but they loved their work, and they talked about it a lot at home, and I was part of all of that. It was like I was an equal partner, and if they discussed ethical things, they asked me what I thought and they respected what I said . . . They never once, not that I can ever recall, told me that they wanted me to go to medical school. They told me that they wanted me to be happy and that the best way to be happy was to find a life's work that contributed something to society and that was meaningful to me. They always said that I could be anything I wanted to be, and they'd always be proud of me, no matter what I did. I didn't seriously consider anything else but medicine, because they seemed so satisfied . . . I wanted to be like them. I wanted them to be as proud of me as I was of them."

He was in the first year of residency training to be an orthopedist, a big-shouldered man who had played football in college for two years before his left knee went bad and he was told he'd run the risk of permanent injury or at least developing arthritis later in life if he continued to play. When he quit, his father was enraged, but, he said, that really didn't surprise him.

"My father always said that you cheated yourself if you didn't play up to par, which was what he called potential. I agree with that in principle, but the problem I had was that he always set my par a lot higher than I thought it should be. The result was that he was disappointed in me much of the time. I made the decision to quit football all by myself, and I was confident that it was the right thing for me to do. But when I told him, you'd have thought that I'd just been convicted of bank robbery. He said that I could have become a starter, maybe a star, if I'd stuck with it. He didn't understand how I could do this to him, after everything he had done for me. . . . I think one of the reasons I went to medical school was to make him proud of me, sort of a compensation for giving up football. . . . Medical school wasn't as hard as I'd heard it was. I finished in the top half of my class, and that disappointed my father, too, but at least he's able to talk about 'my son, the doctor,' and that makes him feel important. I wish I'd had some brothers and sisters. Maybe they could have taken some of the heat off me. . . . He's a nice enough man, in some ways, but he did a number on me as a father, and here I am, becoming a doctor, and I don't even know for sure that this is what I want."

A psychiatrist who is an only child told me that he was started along the road to achievement by parents who "very quietly helped me to feel that I could do it, whatever it was that I wanted to do. My father left copies of *Scientific American* all over the house, and that wasn't by accident. He was a very tidy man, but he left them out where I would see them and be exposed to thinking that would challenge me. I'd pick up a copy, and I'd be thinking 'Gee, I can be the next Einstein.' Then I'd get an A on a science test, and that would be further proof that I was walking in Einstein's shoes. . . . My mother was a musician. She played the violin, and there always seemed to be a violin around for me to play with, and I'd see myself as the next Heifetz. A lot of fantasy took root then. My parents would take me to a museum, and I'd stare at a Picasso and ask them 'Why can't I do that?' And they'd say 'No reason at all.' My fantasy was unlimited. There was no reality to a lot of it, but it provided me with the myth that I was special, that I couldn't be held back from achieving whatever I wanted.

"The price I paid for all of this grandiosity, and that's what it really was, was that I didn't grow up as a balanced person. My social skills were very immature, and I was shy and didn't know how to play with other kids. To this day it's still hard for me to let down my hair and play . . . Play is the work of childhood, and if you don't get enough of it then, it can be traumatic later on . . . There was one time I remember when I was running a group therapy session. I was the leader, and I came in one evening, and everybody was fooling around. They were having a great time, and I felt the same way I felt the first day I went to kindergarten. I didn't have the skills to join in. There was no way I could become part of the fun."

Leon Katz, a judge who is an only child, told me that he is "neurotically prompt, conscientious, achievement-oriented and married to the work ethic. I demand a lot of myself and other people, and so when I'm interviewing applicants for law clerk-ships, I look for people who are willing to give a lot and who want to build a foundation of achievement and success. With me, it's a plus when an applicant is an only child because I know that applicant will be conscientious, perfectionistic, willing to work long hours to achieve the goals. Only children are willing to pay the price for success, and I like that because I paid the price, and I guess we always look for people who are mirror images of ourselves . . . Of course it's not legal to ask applicants if they're only children, but there are ways to find out. I might say 'Tell me about your brothers and sisters,' and then I know. I've found it to be a good barometer of success."

The Other Side

The whole matter of achievement has two sides to it, of course, and some people are not as unrestrained in their enthusiasm as John T. Molloy, a consultant whose name became a household word because of his books about dressing for success. Molloy writes about others things, too, such as success and achievement, and one of his books is entitled *How to Work the Competition Into the Ground and Have Fun Doing It.* It's a book that, to me, glorifies beyond reason the virtues of hard work, long hours and mammoth achievement, and it collides head-on with my personal philosophy that work should be one of many important things in life and that achievement must be weighed against the cost of success before it can be judged to be worthwhile or not. Jonas Salk, in a memorable interview with me many years ago, said that in the process of discovering the polio vaccine, he had become temporarily a one-dimensional person who had no time for relationships or relaxation. He never would allow that to happen to him again, and he always would build in free time as a buffer against the unchecked passion of achievement. I told that story to Molloy, but he wasn't impressed. The drumbeat to which high achievers must march, he proclaimed, is win, win, win because we're in a competitive world and the alternative is to lose, lose, lose.

One of the many people I've met who doesn't share that view is psychiatrist Carl Whitaker, the famed family therapist, who told me that a major problem in families is that "we get no recognition for who we are but only for what we achieve." Until the emphasis is switched, we're doomed to be a nation of people who spend a good bit of time out of control, chasing achievement in a futile attempt to win acceptance and justify our existence.

After my mother died, when I, as the only child, had the tearful task of disposing of the contents of the family home, I found something in a dresser drawer that to this day is a mystery to me.

I have no idea where it came from, this plaque, made of red cedar, on which had been burned these words:

> No amount of success is ever enough; the slightest failure is too much.
>
> —Darrell Sifford

I stood there and stared at it. There was something familiar about it, but surely it was nothing that I would articulate as a life philosophy, not since I renounced workaholism in favor of balance long ago. But then why was it familiar? Suddenly it came to me. In an earlier book I'd written, I had quoted psychiatrist Theodore Isaac Rubin as saying the crazy thing about growing up in America these days is that we're so invested in our work and so identified with it that no amount of success is ever enough and the slightest failure is too much. Somebody had taken the quotation out of context and committed it to indestructible cedar. What did I do with the plaque? When I mentioned it to my son Grant, he asked if he could have it, and today it hangs in the kitchen of his apartment in San Diego. He wanted it, he said, as a daily reality check, in case he ever felt in danger of becoming overly invested in the rat race. So the piece of cedar is doing some good after all, but certainly not in the way that the creator had in mind.

The Risk-Takers

People who are high achievers tend to be risk-takers. They're able to do this because they're so confident of succeeding that they aren't easily spooked by concerns about failing. Psychologist Aaron Hemsley, who by anybody's definition is a risk taker, told me that the ability to take risks without debilitating anxiety stems from "the one basic thing that all risk-takers have, a high level of self-esteem. They are very confident about themselves, and they would score high if you measured them on a self-reliant scale."

Hemsley, who is president of The Behavior Management Group in Orange, California, crisscrosses the nation to deliver his seminars on "the psychology of maximum performance" in what really is a second career for him. In the beginning, he practiced traditional psychology, spending much of his time around troubled, confused, depressed clients. It was a miserable period in his life because he feared that his clients' troubles eventually might rub off and contaminate him. That's when he decided to make the break and take a risk, by specializing in an area that would bring him into regular contact with successful people whose main concern was how to become even more successful and realize more fully the total scope of their potential.

He never seriously considered the possibility that this new direction might fizzle, and this is because he shares with other risk-takers a classic quality: "We're too dumb to know that we can't succeed, so we go ahead and do it. In a sense a prudent person might back off, might say 'Gee, I can't start a new business in this economy.' But a risk-taker says 'This is what I want to do, and I'm going to do it.' The risk-taker says 'I'll start the business now and worry about the economy later.' "

The risk-takers, in Hemsley's opinion, are more successful and more satisfied with their lives than people who play it safe because they seize the initiative and play the game by their own rules. For the most part, people are set up to become risk-takers by their childhood conditioning, he said. "It was the childhood experience that created their sense of confidence, their feeling that they can do it better than anybody else. It also contributed to their lack of need to conform, to consider doing it somebody else's way, by somebody else's standards. There's almost the feeling that 'I don't want to learn about doing it your way because I think my way is better.' And while this may sound haughty, it's part of what makes them so successful and able to achieve so much."

If you lined up a sample of America's risk-takers, you'd find that a high percentage of them are only children and first-born children, said Hemsley. This is because they "are raised with a lot more praise from parents. The first kid does anything, and everybody notices. He crawls, and everybody gets excited. He has four or five photo albums. By the time the fourth or fifth child comes along, nobody notices anything, and this child may have not four or five photo albums but two or three pages in one album. This reflects differences in parents' attitudes and expectations." The result is that this child often lacks the elevated sense of self-esteem that is the fundamental superstructure around which risk-taking develops.

The first child tends to get "a lot of positive feedback from parents that he's good. There are a lot of expectations" that are not disguised, and the child knows that he is expected to be better than others. In a sense he has permission to become a freewheeler, and this is what he does when he takes risks. He thumbs his nose at the odds, because he never seriously considers the possibility that things won't work out. His self-esteem tends to be so strong that he understands the worst thing that can happen is that he'll fail. This is okay because failure can be shaped into a learning experience that will speed success the next time around. People without this level of self-esteem often tend to be frozen into inaction by fear of an undertaking's failure, which they view as being the same as personal failure.

Although the role of parents is important in creating conditions for a child to become a risk-taker, other people can be involved, too, such as peers and teachers. "Once in a while, there is a teacher with whom you come in contact and get a lifetime of positive influence. I've seen a few of these, although most teachers just pass through and are forgotten, without leaving any permanent impact. . . . In the peer group there can be the recognition that you do things better than anybody else, and you get the kind of reinforcement" that makes it possible for you to shoot for the moon.

The Challenge of Change

Philip Bobrove grew up like a lot of only children, well taken care of, and the need to take risks never really presented itself. "From high school I went to a college education that was paid for. Then I went to graduate school with a scholarship and became a psychologist. After that I was into jobs in large institutions that took care of me. I got married. There was no risk because I married somebody with the same interests, somebody from the same class. I had children because I was supposed to have children."

In 1981 he was clinical director of the geriatrics division of Jefferson Medical College's department of psychiatry and human behavior. He was, in his words, "Peter Principled in my administrative ability. I reached a certain point and it was obvious that I didn't have the drive to continue. I enjoyed the clinical work, but what needed to be done administratively—the writing of grant applications and things like that—didn't interest me. To me the paperwork was like a Rube Goldberg machine that had lots of movement but that did zero. I wanted to get out."

It was a decision that, at the time, figured to cost him $10,000 a year, but he wanted to expand his limited private practice. "Being my own man is worth more to me than money. Having time to talk with my wife before 11:00 P.M. is worth more to me than money." He was taking what he called the first risk of his life, going from full-time to half-time at the college, losing many of his benefits and the tuition reimbursement that his three sons would have been eligible to receive. "I could have continued where I was. I really had a choice. My boss always had been supportive of me, and he could have made it easy for me to continue, but I couldn't. For myself, I needed a change."

He bought a seventy-five-year-old house in Haddonfield, New Jersey, where he set up his office, and he rented out the rest of the space. "Yes, it's a risk," he repeated. "I'm an economic idiot. If I balance my checkbook, I feel like a genius. I was very insulated from all of that when I worked at the medical college. My salary came in regularly; I knew how much I would earn; I didn't have to worry about repairs because the big daddy in the sky took care of all of that."

Was it a kind of midlife crisis that had prompted him to act at this time, when he was forty-five? In a sense that's what it was, he said, "although I don't like to call it that because it cheapens it, like if I can identify it, it will go away. I'm not saying I'm going to run off with a twenty-six-year-old blonde, but I know what I can do. I know my skills." The midlife crisis comes when we arrive at the point at which we seriously ask ourselves what life is really worth, he said. "I now have less time to live than I've already lived. I wasn't happy with my life. . . . There was the realization that this was what I wanted to do, that I was really good. I felt competent, and I was moving from a position where I felt mediocre as an administrator."

It is not prudent, he said, for anybody to take a risk as major as his "unless the unhappiness is pervasive in everything you do, unless you have a burning desire to do this new thing. . . . But if you're where I was, at the point where the work no longer is meaningful and rewarding, then you've got to weigh the risks of continuing the work and dropping dead of boredom . . . or running out on your wife, smashing yourself up or drinking too much. If you're going to do that, then it's better to try to channel yourself into something constructive," such as a new job. It's important to recognize that a certain amount of luck is involved in successfully negotiating most changes. But it's not luck in the sense that "a bundle of cash drops out of a truck, and you pick it up. No, luck is being around and taking advantage of things that happen. . . . People say 'Gee, Phil, you were lucky that the house came on the market when you needed it, but I'd been looking for a house just like it." In other words, he helped make his own luck, and that's the best kind.

It's apparent to him that most of us have far more control over our lives than we often think. "It may be true that we're like a leaf blowing in the wind, but we can change direction, a little anyway. We're not helpless victims of destiny."

Whatever happened to Philip Bobrove? A year and a half later, he looked like a man who had been injected with high-octane fuel. He called it a new direction in life. "I've learned about economics. My accountant gives me orders—deduct this, depreciate that— and I think the government and I are in an excellent partnership now. I've reached a point economically that I never thought was possible." His private practice had spurted and he had done much better than he expected in such a short time. But it hadn't all been a cakewalk. In the beginning, even though he sometimes had more work than he could do, "I still worried . . . crazy worries. I'd think 'Well, next week will be it. I'll go down to four hours, and they'll foreclose on me.' But it never happened. As one patient left, another came in, usually on a referral from somebody who felt good about therapy."

Buying the seven-room house had weighed heavily on him. "I've never been so far in debt. I had a lot of sleepless nights. I'd lie there and think 'What am I doing? Where will I get the money?' But it all worked out. In an overall sense, I have zero regrets. I exchanged one bag of problems for another, but they're problems I can deal with, problems on a human scale." What he called "the biggest plus" is waking up every morning and saying "How do you do, boss?" He never had liked working for other people. In fact, he said, "I hate it when somebody tells me to do something. This is unreasonable, I know, and sometimes very maladaptive, but I hate it. Yet I can tell myself to do something, and I don't mind it. If I have to work until one in the morning because I decide that I have to, I don't mind it. But if somebody told me I had to, that would be something else."

These days Bobrove is a full-fledged entrepreneur. He has trimmed his ties to the medical school to a thread, expanded his practice to the limit that he wants, bought another house that he rents to therapists and business people. And he's very much in control of his life.

A while back he invited me to accompany him on a sunny fall day to trek through the New Jersey pine barrens, an area so rural that he needed a geological survey map to guide us along the dirt roads, past the uncharted ponds, the long-ago-deserted log cabins, the little white church in the middle of nowhere. There we were, two only children, wading in a cranberry bog and eating raw cranberries. We stared in awe at a silent river that looked as it must have two hundred fifty years ago, the water crystal clear and potable. He pulled a poncho from the back of his four-wheel-drive van and we sat on the river bank under a pine tree, munched on tuna pita sandwiches and sipped white zinfandel out of tin cups. I'd never experienced anything like this before, so different from my life on the thirty-seventh floor of a condominium in the heart of the city, as if we had dropped down from space and landed smack-dab in another culture. "Phil," I said finally, "this is what it's all about, isn't it?"

He didn't respond, but I heard him anyway.

The "Special" Achiever

Psychiatrist Pirooz Sholevar was explaining that only children who are made to feel special at home become "very good at re-creating this situation in other areas, especially at school. They get teachers to adopt them, just like parents, and to give them special treatment, to treat them as exceptional." These are the teachers under whom only children tend to spread their wings and fly high and far because they want to be as great as the teachers expect them to be.

That's the good side of it. The other side is that these only children, regardless of how bright they are, tend not to do so well when they're with teachers who treat them just like everybody else. When they're lumped in with all the others, only children may complain to their parents that the teacher is very mean. What they may be saying is that the teachers don't treat them as well as their parents, don't go out of their way to satisfy them all the time. If there's one thing that an only child who feels special at home can't tolerate at school or anywhere else, for that matter, it's benign neglect. It's important for parents to understand this.

I was speaking before a group of educators about the role teachers play in shaping students, and I reminisced about the two teachers who had the biggest impact on my development in high school, who put fire into my heart and belief into my soul, who spent extra time with me, who listened patiently to my unending stream of questions, who gave me answers and, most of all, the confidence that I had within me whatever it would take to do whatever I wanted.

First, there was Francille Bailey, Miss B, the newspaper adviser, who believed and taught me that the best writing was simple writing. She made anything fun, even reading convoluted English literature, because she thought that life should be fun. I worked hard for her, not so much because she demanded it but because I liked her so much and didn't want to disappoint her. She knew what was important at the moment, even if it really didn't mean anything in the long run, and she let you know that she knew it was important.

On a Friday morning in November, when I was a senior and captain of the football team, I sat in her classroom and stared out the window when I should have been writing on a test. We had a game that night, and our team and the team we were playing were both undefeated, and the winner would be invited to the Missouri Show-Me Bowl, which was, in our judgment, the biggest thing in the world. I was wondering if I'd be able to get away from their clawing tackles to run my pass patterns, and I didn't even want to think about the test that was in front of me. Miss B intuitively understood my dilemma. She walked casually to my desk at the back of the room and whispered, "Don't worry, you can do it Monday." Is that special treatment?

A few years ago I was back home to speak during Journalism Week at the University of Missouri, and the first call that came to my hotel room was from Miss B. She had made arrangements to attend the dinner at which I was speaking, and said she'd like to stop by, have a drink with me and then give me a ride. It was a beautiful evening. She sat with me at dinner and, when I introduced her during my speech, the audience gave her a standing ovation, which I thought was entirely appropriate.

My second great teacher was Stella Hellman, a frail-looking little lady who had taught for more years than anybody could imagine. She had a reputation, and it was well-deserved, of being the toughest, most demanding teacher in the school. It also was widely believed that she discriminated against football players because she believed them to be dumbbells who were incapable of anything more creative than butting heads. The courses she taught could be taken only as electives, and the consensus among students was that her courses were so terrifying that it would be unfair to assign anybody to them.

When she got mad, everybody said, she resorted to the ultimate dirty word in her vocabulary: *Piffle!* Students at whom the ultimate dirty word was hurled might as well pack their books and leave, because they were doomed. I signed up for her advanced grammar course, and on the first day she looked at me over her wire-rimmed glasses and wanted to know what I was doing there. I told her that I was going to be a writer, that I wanted the best foundation in grammar that I could get, that I passionately believed she could help me.

We had a great year together. I diagrammed sentences until my fingers and my brain went numb, but I learned what precision grammar was all about. I think she learned something about football players, too—that without our helmets we were pretty much like everybody else. She was a grand lady who didn't hesitate to stay after class, if I asked her, to explain again why the modifier went here instead of there.

The educators liked those stories about my favorite teachers. Somebody in the back row raised a hand and asked why I had bonded so closely and quickly to the two women. My response was out of my mouth before I realized what I had said: "They made me feel special. They treated me just like my parents."

Voices That Come in the Night . . . and Day

The high-achieving only child is at risk of developing what amounts to a backlash that, at times, can make him doubt that the good times are going to last. After he went into private practice Philip Bobrove, you'll recall, said a tape that played and replayed in his mind was: "Well, next week will be it. I'll go down to four hours, and they'll foreclose on me." A more severe message that is experienced by many, no matter how fully they have paid their dues to get where they are, goes something like this: "You're not good enough, and one of these days everybody will find out, and then it'll all be over." It's a message that makes it impossible for many high-achievers to enjoy or even recognize their success. It's a message that makes them feel like impostors.

Pauline Rose Clance grew up in the poverty of the Appalachian mountains in a culture in which nobody historically received much, if any, formal education. But she cracked the mold, although she lived with an impending sense of failure as an undergraduate student. No, she never failed—to the contrary, she ranked high in her class—but no amount of success seemed sufficient to put her fears to rest.

Then she went into an intensely competitive graduate program in psychology at the University of Kentucky. Her fear level rocketed, and she found herself sharing her concerns with friends: "I can't possibly make it. I'll flunk this big exam and that'll be it. They'll throw me out of school." But the more she worried, the better her academic record became, and her friends began to ask what was going on: "Look, Pauline, we want to be supportive, but this stuff is irritating us. How do we know when we really need to be concerned if you're always crying wolf? What's the matter with you?"

The confrontation forced her to take a look at what was happening, and when she looked, this is what she found: "An exam would come up, and I'd worry, suffer from extreme anxiety, maybe even have nightmares about failing. I'd study hard, really hard, and then in the exam I'd do well. The strange thing was that my very success was reinforcing the cycle. I had to worry to be successful. If I didn't worry, I might fail."

It sounded crazy, but she accepted it as the way things were. After all, when you grow up in the mountains, you're bound to be a little insecure, bound to worry about failing. Yes, that was it, her background. That explained everything. But then, a few years later, a strange thing happened. Pauline Clance was now a teacher at Oberlin College, and seemed constantly to encounter students whose fears paralleled her own. "I'd see kids with sky-high SAT scores, kids who were doing fine in school, and they were convinced that their next failure was just around the corner. They'd say things like 'I don't feel I belong here with all these intelligent people.' I'd ask how they got into such a good school, and they'd say 'The admissions committee made a mistake.' I'd ask how they were able to make such high scores, and they'd say 'I'm good at multiple-choice tests.' What they could do with ease they felt had nothing to do with intelligence. What they had to struggle to do became their baseline for intelligence. They were every bit as fearful of failure as I'd been, and still was."

She began to talk to her colleagues. Yes, they were seeing this irrational fear in many of their students, too. And, to be honest, the colleagues were a bit fearful themselves, fearful that they didn't belong, that they weren't good enough, that sooner or later they would be *exposed*. She took her questions off campus and into the business world, where she found that many businesspeople, no matter how successful they were, voiced the belief that their success was based on luck or something other than their ability and that failure surely was staring them in the eye. What was going on? Everybody, it seemed, felt like an impostor.

Pauline Rose Clance became professor of psychology at George State University, continued her study of the high-achieving people who felt that they would fail and eventually wrote *The Impostor Phenomenon.* Here are four common elements that she has found in people who feel they are impostors:

· A discrepancy in feedback that the child receives from the family and from teachers, friends and others outside the family. "The child doesn't know which messages to believe. Since the child's very survival in the world is dependent upon his or her family, the child is torn by the inconsistent images that apparently are being seen."

· Heavy emphasis in the family on the child's being able to learn quickly and "to maneuver well in the world. Often stories are told about aunts, uncles, cousins or friends and whether or not these people have been bright enough to get ahead and make something of themselves. From a very early age, the child understands that it is valuable to be smart."

· The child's perception that his abilities are different from the rest of the family's abilities. Example: A child is talented in math, but nobody else can add much more than two and two. "The child begins to feel that he or she is different and even begins to feel like the proverbial square peg trying to fit in the family's round hole."

· Lack of praise. "Some parents may brag to friends and relatives about what their child has done, but they rarely let the child know how proud they are of achievements." Reasons for this lack of praise vary from the parents' fearing that the child may become arrogant to the parents' seeing no need for praise because the child is simply equaling their high expectations. This can be a hook that especially puts the only child at increased risk.

Clance said that prime times for impostor feelings to emerge most strongly involve major life events—entering college or graduate school, taking the first job, getting a major promotion, having the first child. "It helps to know when these feelings are most likely to occur. It helps to know that, when they do occur, you're not alone. What you're feeling is not an abnormality" but a condition that seemingly grips masses of the population. Interviews with successful businesspeople in California showed that seventy percent at times felt like impostors.

What is the treatment to help people enjoy the fruits of their achievements? "It helps just to know that you suffer from the impostor phenomenon. It helps to label it, to know that others have the same problem. It helps to know that what you feel represents not reality but fears. History shows that you have succeeded. . . . For some people this is enough" to set them free. For others therapy is needed. "It gets them to look at why they're holding onto it. What's the benefit? What would happen if they didn't feel this way? Why are they afraid of success? Why do they feel guilty about success?" A classic payoff for being an impostor is that "you don't have to deal with the guilt of success if you say that you're not that successful."

Too Much, Too Soon

Other people are unable to enjoy their success not because they feel like impostors but because their achievements have come too quickly. Once again, only children are at increased risk because they're often programmed to run so fast to reach their goals that they sometimes succeed before they're emotionally ready to handle it. What happens to them is that they can get hit with an authentic midlife crisis when they're well short of middle age.

John Reckless practices psychiatry in Durham, North Carolina, and he was telling me that for a long time he held the notion that midlife crisis came "to a man in his forties with an aging marital relationship, a man who had worked hard to acquire success, who got to the top of the heap and who became unhappy. I had the idea that this was a function of the number of years of life. I now believe that this is not true. I'm seeing more and more men in their middle thirties" and even younger who are struggling through their crises.

"I'm seeing as a patient a man who is twenty-eight and who told me 'I'm now where I expected to be at fifty-five, and I can't handle it.' He's intelligent and he's dying of depression. He's aware already that it's not true that if he keeps going, one day he'll find a golden sunset and be happy. It's just not there." The so-called midlife crisis is "not an occurrence of the middle years but a function of making it to the top and finding that what you're seeking is not there. Because men are making it to the top earlier these days, the crisis is coming earlier."

Reckless said that he hadn't changed his thoughts about what it takes to resolve the crisis, at whatever age it strikes. The solution remains coming to terms with yourself and "changing expectations so that you don't have to be the most successful or the wealthiest . . . and so that you can invest in personal relationships."

6

Forgive and Forget: Why Making Up Is Hard to Do

While I've made undeniable progress over the years in toning down my need to be perfect and putting a rein on my unreasonable drive to achieve, I have not done so well in the area that is the subject of this chapter. I am not very good at forgiving and forgetting. I tend to carry grudges and, in the language of therapists, I collect "brown stamps," the reminders of life's injustices. When I'm crossed, taken advantage of, treated unfairly, I file the event away in my memory bank, which compounds interest daily. Later, when the appropriate key is pushed into the lock, I haul it out—and there it is, with all the freshness of a bagel that has been taken out of the deep freeze and thawed. I'm a scorekeeper, and I could have been the author of a bumper sticker that I saw not long ago: "I don't forget; I get even." It's not a part of me that I want to keep, and I've worked to get rid of it, but it's still there, in all its chilling ugliness.

Why? I think it's part of the legacy of the only child, and a lot of us have the problem. Knowing that we have each other for company does not, by itself, help us one bit, but it does make us feel less alone, and that's surely worth something.

Molly has been married to Ken, who is an only child, for a decade. She's one of six children, and she long ago mastered the art of forgiving and forgetting. "It was part of my survival training as a kid growing up," she told me. "Somebody was having a fight with somebody every day, and we had to learn not to carry it around forever, to talk it out, turn it loose. By bedtime, usually by supper, we had buried the hatchet, and we could laugh about it. My mother and father taught us this by example. They weren't very verbal and they weren't very affectionate with each other in front of the kids, but whenever they had a disagreement, they always made up and hugged, no matter where they were, no matter who was around. My mother, right before I got married, had a mother-daughter talk with me, and I assumed it was going to be about sex, but it wasn't. She said 'The most important thing I can tell you about being married is that you never should go to bed angry.' What she meant, of course, was that whatever caused the anger should be dealt with sooner rather than later. It was good advice, but the problem is that I'm married to a guy who makes it very difficult for me. . . . It's hard to forgive and forget when Ken keeps track of everything that ever went wrong. He can't turn loose of the stuff. . . . He has a memory like an elephant. Five years after something happens, he brings it back up and uses it against me, as if it had happened yesterday."

What makes it so difficult for Ken to forgive and forget? His explanation is interesting, even if it doesn't necessarily give you a warm feeling about the man. "There's a saying 'Fool me once, shame on you; fool me twice, shame on me.' I don't intend to let anybody make a fool of me. I don't ever want to be in a position in which I have to say 'Gee, I should have known better.' I don't intend to let anybody put anything over on me, and the best way to do that is to remember who tried to do it, how they tried and what their motivation was. . . . I don't try to make life difficult for Molly, but, by God, she's got to understand that she can't do this stuff to me and then say 'Aw, Ken, honey, I'm sorry,' and that's the end of it. I don't want a pound of flesh. I'm not into revenge. I'm into protecting myself, and the way I know how to do that is to remember. I'm good at remembering."

Why is Ken good at remembering? It should come as no surprise that Ken's parents remembered, too. With what seemed to be a painful effort, Ken recalled those early years. "They argued a lot, but they never seemed to settle anything. The stuff just went on and on, and it was like they'd pause between rounds to get their breath before they started again. If the toast got burned on Monday morning, he still was telling her about it on Friday afternoon. If he had too much to drink or stayed out too late on Saturday, she still was scolding him a month from Sunday. They fought, but they never settled anything. If there had been a community college course back then in conflict resolution, they should have been the first two people to sign up." Ken said that he didn't "harp like that to Molly. I like to resolve things, but it's just that I tend to remember things and then I bring them back up when I need to, when what's happening today seems like part of a pattern from the past."

It's difficult for a lot of us, whether or not we're only children, to forgive and forget. It seems almost to be a quality of being human, to remember, to hang on, to carry grudges. Lewis Smedes, a clergyman, wrote a book about it and described forgiveness to me as "so damned unnatural." It's a special problem of only children, for at least two reasons. The first, as we've just heard from Molly, is that we didn't have much opportunity to practice when we were growing up. In families with several children, the children clash with each other but learn to put it behind them. Like Molly, they've usually resolved their conflicts before bedtime, and tomorrow is another day. The slate has been wiped clean, free of the debris from today.

But it's different for the only child. If we fight with a playmate, we can hold onto our sense of righteousness because we don't have to go home with him, eat dinner with him, share a bathroom with him. If we want to, we can cross him off our list altogether and find another playmate. We don't have an investment in him that is so great that we *must* make up, mend our fences and go from there. This is an important area of learning in which the only child so often gets shortchanged. We literally don't learn how to make up.

Because of our relative isolation—usually it's the three of us, our parents and ourselves—we fight mostly with our parents. In healthy families, the parents take the initiative in forgiving and forgetting. "You have behaved badly, Johnny, and I'm disappointed, but I love you and I forgive you." Or "Sarah, I realize now that I was unreasonable in what I said to you earlier, and I apologize. I'm really sorry." This is a mark of exceptional parenting, and, if we're lucky, we've been exposed to it and to some extent we can model our behavior after it. If we had parents who disagreed in front of us and who then made up, like Molly's parents, we have seen firsthand the process of forgiving and forgetting. Unfortunately, however, it doesn't compensate adequately for our not having been in a position in which we literally were compelled to initiate the process ourselves. We were not prepared, as fully as children with siblings, for the adult process of forgiving and forgetting.

What can we do? A lot of therapists suggest that we practice, practice, practice. We anticipate the next disagreement with somebody who matters to us, and we rehearse what we're going to say and how we're going to say it. It's difficult at first. It feels clumsy. But it does get easier with practice, and it can help us patch that large hole in our bag of skills. We'll feel better, and so will those around us.

The second reason why only children have trouble with forgiving and forgetting is that they get tripped up by their own grandiosity. We think we're great and when other people don't always agree, we get mad at them. We are victimized by what therapists call a "core myth," a belief about ourselves and the world that, whether it's real or imagined, shapes to a great extent the way we feel and act. It can color our view, obscure our vision, make enemies of friends, turn victory into defeat. There are many core myths, and here's a story that illustrates one of them:

The man's car breaks down late at night on a country road. He remembers that he saw a farmhouse about a mile back, so he starts to walk there because he needs to telephone for help. As he walks, he thinks that he'll have to wake up the farmer to ask to use the phone. The farmer probably will be irate, maybe even nasty. The farmer's wife won't like it either, and she'll put in her two cents, too. The dog will bark, maybe even bite. As he approaches the house, the man is certain that his request will be refused, and he's frustrated and angry. He knocks on the door, and when the farmer answers, the man screams "I wouldn't use your damn phone if you begged me!" Then he stalks back to his car and curses the circumstances that have caused him to be stranded in the middle of nowhere, all alone, without any help.

The most common core myths for many of us, said psychiatrist Alan Summers, are these: "I'm a failure; I'm doomed to eternal deprivation; I'll never be able to get my needs met; I'm helpless to do anything about the way the world treats me." The man with the broken-down car obviously believed that he wasn't going to be helped and proceeded to behave in a way that guaranteed he wouldn't be. But he had ample "evidence" that it wasn't his fault. After all, the farmer wouldn't have come to his aid anyway, to his way of thinking.

The overriding core myth of the only child is "I am extra special." It's a myth that well-intentioned parents often help construct by giving the only child too much gratification and not enough frustration, too much rope and not enough limitation. The only child buys into it but then runs into difficulty when people in the outside world don't treat him as "special enough" to satisfy his needs. This is when the only child may put up a barrier, as protection against narcissistic injury.

Carrying the Grudge: Why?

The barrier is a grudge, and it holds people at a distance and keeps intact the core myth. This is a major part of what makes it so difficult for only children to forgive and forget. The grudge gets in the way. The grudge is like a wall between the only child and the core myth. It prevents the only child from rubbing up against the myth in such an abrasive way that he is forced to confront it and modify it. What happens in good therapy is that the wall is torn down and the core myth is exposed, examined, understood, changed into something more realistic and workable.

Where is the line drawn between the core myth of being special, which is a heavy cross to bear, and healthy self-esteem, which is essential if we're to be happy, successful people? I agree with the therapists who put it this way: We should recognize ourselves as unique people with unique talents. Our obligation is to develop our talents as much as possible and communicate them to the world. But the world is under no obligation to applaud us. If we go unrecognized, we can't hold it against the world. We've done what we were supposed to do, fulfilled our task. We can do no more. Leonardo da Vinci—who was an only child—shared what he had with the world even though he died without feeling recognized or appreciated. It's the same story with the artists and writers who, although they weren't acclaimed until much later, never stopped making their statements through their work.

How can we learn to forgive and forget, to surrender our grudges? The first step is recognizing that we need to change. For many of us, the first step is the hardest.

A Blueprint for Change

Lewis Smedes, professor of theology and ethics at Fuller Theological Seminary in Pasadena, California, told me that forgiveness is a hard concept to sell because it swims against the tide of human nature. "It's natural to think of getting even when somebody has hurt you. That's the moral way. It's fair and just. Forgiving is suspicious, revolutionary, in violation of the moral order. . . . It comes down to the difference between justice and vengeance, a difference that's tough to digest. I never met anybody who sought vengeance who didn't think that he was seeking justice. But vengeance is a desire for 'justice' to satisfy your own need for healing. 'I want you to suffer so I will have the satisfaction of knowing you hurt as much as I.' The problem with that kind of 'justice' is that it's a loser's game. . . . If I seek the justice of equal pain, I'll never get it. In the pain game I never get even because I, as the injured person, weigh pain on a different scale than the person who inflicted the pain on me. The pain is not quantified the same way, so I never get the satisfaction I'm seeking."

The only real satisfaction, in Smedes' mind, comes from the cleansing offered by the act of forgiveness. This is what frees us from the pain of the past, and in that sense we clearly forgive others to benefit ourselves, not those who have hurt us. In his book

Forgive & Forget, published in 1984, Smedes described four stages of the forgiveness process:

· *Hurt.* "When somebody causes you pain so deep and unfair that you cannot forget it, you are pushed into the first stage of the crisis of forgiving. . . . The hurt that creates a crisis of forgiving has three dimensions. It always is personal, unfair and deep. When you feel this kind of three-dimensional pain, you have a wound that can be healed only by forgiving the one who wounded you."

· *Hate.* "You cannot shake the memory of how much you were hurt, and you cannot wish your enemy well. You sometimes want the person who hurt you to suffer as you are suffering. . . . Hate eventually needs healing. Passive or aggressive, hate is a malignancy. It surely hurts the hater more than it hurts the hated. We must not confuse hate with anger. It is hate and not anger that needs healing. Anger is a sign that we are alive and well. Hate is a sign that we are sick and need to be healed."

· *Healing.* "You are given 'magic eyes' to see the person who hurt you in a new light. Your memory is healed, and you turn back the flow of pain and are free again. . . . When you forgive . . . you perform spiritual surgery inside your soul. You cut away the wrong . . . and you see your 'enemy' through the magic eyes that can heal your soul. Detach that person from the hurt and let it go, then invite that person back into your mind, fresh, as if a piece of history between the two of you has been rewritten, its grip on your memory broken."

· *Coming together.* If the person you invited back into your life returns with honesty, "love can move you both toward a new and healed relationship. The fourth stage depends on the person you forgive as much as it depends on you. Sometimes that person doesn't come back, and you have to be healed alone. You start over . . . in the semidarkness of partial understanding. You probably will never understand why you were hurt. But forgiving is not having to understand."

What happens to people who don't ever forgive? Smedes said that he preferred to talk in reference to himself. "When I don't forgive, I find that my resentment and hate get so mixed up with my pain. In not forgiving, I replay the painful tape over again . . . and I let the person who hurt me once clobber me over and over again. I perpetuate the pain, and I spread it to other people. I don't try to get even with the person who hurt me, but I make others the target. I become impatient with my children, surly, unpleasant with my wife. When I'm not forgiving, I feel so damned self-righteous. I never feel so virtuous as when I feel hurt." But that's a dead-end road because in the long run, it accomplishes nothing—except showering more pain on everybody.

I asked Smedes how many times we should forgive somebody who wrongs us. Even a peaceful man like Shane, in the classic movie, could put up with only so much. Smedes had a thought-provoking answer that made me feel almost foolish for having brought up the question:

"It's a huge mistake to think of forgiveness as an obligation. It's not a duty, not a way to be nice to the rotten person who's gotten us into this mess. It's a bad mistake to think of forgiveness as toleration or to equate forgiveness with putting up with stuff, with being a doormat. If you think of forgiveness as a willingness to suffer, then that gets us into this kind of question—about how many times you can forgive somebody. But if you think of forgiveness, first of all, as a way to deal with yourself, to get freedom from the past, then the question changes in texture. How much are you willing to put up with and still maintain the same relationship with the other person? Any relationship has to have as a basis the element of truthfulness. When I forgive you, I remove the obstacle that you put in the way of our relating fully. When I forgive, do I welcome you back into my life? Only with the condition of truth, only if you're willing to be truthful with the fact that you hurt me, that you feel my pain, only if you're truthful with the future and make a believable promise that you don't intend to let this happen again. If I'm dealing with repetition of the hurts you give me, there comes a moment when I say 'Hey, we don't have truthfulness here, and if you clobber me again, we'll have to change the ground rules of the relationship.' And you may have to call it quits."

What if the person you forgive rejects your forgiveness?

That's the other person's right, and we must respect it. "Some say that forgiveness is an act of arrogance. In a sense, it always is, because if I forgive you, it means I've already judged you. It's the other person's freedom to tell me to flush my forgiveness down the toilet, to insist that he's done nothing to be forgiven for. But I can't let the other person control my life, glue me forever to the past" by refusing to accept forgiveness. "For me, forgiveness is a way to claim my right to be healed of pain that I didn't deserve in the first place."

The Big D: Disappointment

Phyllis said that she was struggling with "life's deep hurts and deep disappointments . . . I'm talking about the hurts and disappointments that are inflicted upon us by close friends and our own families—a spouse who has betrayed his or her spouse, children who have disappointed us by not being all that they could be, young adult children who have made moral choices that offend us." She wondered how to deal with her pain, how to forgive and forget and get on with her life, even as she recognized that there inevitably would be more pain, more disappointment.

It helps to be realistic. One of the things that we should be made aware of in early life is that we must expect disappointments. Life can't be made perfect for us, and we must be able to accept that things sometimes turn sour. It's a stressful situation to be disappointed, but if we know enough about the character of people, we will know that they have the potential to disappoint us. When we're disappointed, we should consider that it may be due to the makeup of the individual and not take it as a specific attack on us but the kind of attack that the individual makes on everybody.

We also have to look at what part we may have had in creating our disappointment. This often is very painful. In the words of psychiatrist Spurgeon English "husbands and wives are frail people and open to temptation. If we are going to forgive them, we must have the capacity to see and appreciate their good qualities as well as their weaker ones. We also must bear in mind that whatever they do, they may be doing for themselves rather than against the spouse. To ask 'How could he do this to me?' is an acceptable question, but it also introduces the question 'How could I have prevented this?' Psychologically, we have to bear in mind that the person who continues to carry hurt from others hurts himself in the long run more than he does anything to punish the offender. Rarely does the offender know much or care much about the feelings of the offended. Bitterness is destructive to peace of mind. The hurt one is saying 'I should have received better.' Of course, he should have, but we live in an imperfect world inhabited by imperfect people."

The feeling that we deserve better than we're getting, which invites us to hang onto our grievances, is almost native to the human personality. It's linked to narcissism and self-centeredness, and it's with us from the very beginning. English said that "the trouble comes when parents leave it there, like an old stump on the property. They deplore the stump, but they don't remove it or do anything to make it look better." I asked English what we should do if we've looked within ourselves as well as at the people who have disappointed us. What if we're aware of what we contributed to our disappointment? What if we understand all of this and clean up our act? But what if we're still disappointed because those who matter continue to pepper us with slings and arrows?

English had a marvelous answer—marvelous because it can be translated to mean anything you want it to mean. "You should consider moving to a safer spot, and there is usually one available."

The Biggest Bite of All: Forgiving Ourselves

If we're perfectionistic but fall short of being perfect, how can we ever forgive ourselves? If we don't achieve everything that we've gone after, how can we make peace with ourselves about that? If we've hurt others, how can we ease the burden that we carry on our backs? Again, this is something that unduly plagues only children because they expect so much of themselves.

A psychiatrist told me that he and an only-child patient who was a compulsive gambler had reached an impasse in therapy because the patient wouldn't forgive himself. "He had gambled away his son's inheritance from the grandparents, and he kept saying 'I did a terrible thing,' and treatment got stuck. It's as if he's forever carrying a grudge against himself."

Lewis Smedes described self-forgiveness as "outrageous" in the sense that we must overcome so many formidable obstacles before we're able to do it. "To forgive yourself takes high courage. Who are you, after all, to shake yourself free from the undeniable sins of your private history, as if what you once did has no bearing on who you are now? Where do you get the right to forgive yourself when other people would want you to crawl in shame if they really knew?" The answer, said Smedes, is that "you get the right to forgive yourself only from the entitlements of love. And you dare forgive yourself only with the courage of love. Love is the ultimate source of both your right and your courage to ignore the indictment you level at yourself. When you live as if yesterday's wrong is irrelevant to how you feel about yourself today, you are gambling on a love that frees you even from self-condemnation," although others may continue to condemn you.

Self-forgiveness is the foundation on which is constructed much of the therapy for anguished veterans of the war in Vietnam. Here is David Grady, who, after his combat tour ended when he lost a leg, went back to school and became a psychologist: "I was in an area where most of the casualties were from booby traps and mines. The villagers knew about them. . . . Many of my friends were killed. That doesn't make you feel warmly toward the local people. Why didn't they tell us? We were there supposedly to help them. The answer, of course, was that if they had told us, they would have been killed by guerrillas. But at the time . . . There's a lack of control on carnage in war. And after the war you're left with who you are, with the loss of control . . . What it comes down to eventually is your relationship with yourself. You have to be able to forgive yourself, entertain the idea that things were different then. You have to wash the blood of the enemy off your hands . . . and the blood of the men you loved. It's acceptance. The final step is acceptance. The biggest tragedy is to go on and to be hurt by what happened many years ago—and to hurt others."

Lewis Smedes told me that self-forgiveness hinges on our being able to say and to believe that the past is the past. "I'm sorry about it. But it's not material to what I am now and how I feel now. Who gives somebody the right to take that position? I believe that God gives us that right, through love that makes it possible for us to burn our moral bridges behind us."

7

Praise: The Two-Edged Sword

All of us, adults and children alike, need praise, but to be most helpful, praise should come to us in the right amounts, at the right times, for the right reasons. This is ideal, and it enables us to feel good about ourselves, fulfill some of our dreams of achievement, and share ourselves with the world.

Even praise that is less than ideal can be helpful, too. Later in this chapter you'll read that too much praise can be damaging, but at times, for some people, praise that is spread on as thick as peanut butter can bring a good result. Phillip is an example of somebody who was praised excessively but who used it as a springboard to professional success. A physician with a national reputation, he told me about his growing-up years:

"I was bright, and, as the only child, I got much attention and more praise than you can imagine. The fallout from that was I never thought I was good enough. I thought the praise was out of proportion to whatever I'd done, way too much, and I struggled with the level of expectation in myself that grew out of this. I felt pressure to perform, to be worthy of all that praise. Even today, there are some leftovers from this. I'll be waiting for an appointment, and I'll be pacing and telling myself 'I'm wasting time; I should be doing something.' That's the negative side of it, which causes me to be compulsive about getting things done. But the positive side is that I do get things done. Without tons of praise when I was growing up, I would not be where I am today."

Yes, the only child does tend to get a lot of praise. That's both the good news and the bad news. When I was growing up, I got from my parents enough praise to help me feel that I could climb the highest mountain without pausing to take a breath. I was very confident. In fact, you could say I had a confidence level that at times made it difficult for me to be realistic about myself and other people. I remember one time in my seventh-grade gym class when sides were being chosen for a softball game. Normally, the coach picked me as one of the captains, but on this occasion he didn't, and I was lined up against the wall with everybody else as the two captains began the selection process. In whatever sport we played, on the few times when I wasn't captain, I was accustomed to being picked first, but on this day I was picked second. I couldn't believe it. I stood there and thought, quite sincerely, "That guy didn't pick me first; he's too dumb to be captain of a team." It never occurred to me that not everybody's opinion of me was as high as my own.

Later—quite a few years later—I developed a passionate interest in a young woman, but she didn't return my interest. As a matter of fact, she seemed to go out of her way to let me know that she had done just fine without me for some time and would continue to do so. I just couldn't understand that. Never in my whole life had somebody toward whom I had made an overture failed to respond. I thought about it . . . and concluded "She must be a lesbian." To me there was no other explanation that made sense.

I shared those two stories with child psychiatrist Selma Kramer, who roared with laughter. "Good heavens, that's marvelous," she assured me. "What a remarkable level of self-confidence." Then she turned serious. "Feeling special is important, but it fails to protect you from some realities of life." I understood perfectly what she meant. One of these realities is that not everybody is as enthusiastic about me and my talents as I am.

I found that out early in my newspaper career, and it almost cost me my job. As I reflect on it now, I think that I should have been fired. What happened was this: I was city editor, working for an editor who came off the editorial page and who hadn't had much experience in producing a daily newspaper. I didn't like the way our front page looked. I thought we were mired in tradition to the point that we appeared stodgy, and I took it upon myself to change that. One day, without consulting anybody, I went to a radically different horizontal design with bold headlines that, in my judgment, put zing into our product. The editor didn't share that judgment.

"What the hell have you done?" he asked.

"I've brought this newspaper into the twentieth century."

"Don't you think we should have talked about this?"

"What's to talk about? If you don't like this, we can try something else."

"How about if we don't try anything else right now? How about if we go back to the way it was?"

He seemed reasonably cool, but I was absolutely furious, and, in those days, when I was absolutely furious, I talked before I thought.

"Your problem," I told the editor, "is that you don't know how to make this newspaper better, but I do, and you can't tolerate that."

He put down his pipe and stared at me for what seemed like an eternity. "You know," he said finally, "I'm going to pretend that I never heard you say that." He picked up the pipe by the bowl and pointed the stem at my Adam's apple. "But I'm not very good at pretending, and if you ever say anything like that again, I'm sure that I will hear you, and I'm sure that if I do hear you, I will fire you. Do we have an understanding?"

Yes, we had an understanding about that reality of life.

Psychiatrist Paul Fink said that it's important for parents to praise their child for what he actually does—rather than express disappointment for the child's failing to meet their expectations of what he should do.

"I had this family in therapy—mother, father and four-year-old daughter—and the parents were debating about buying the child an easel. The father said 'I don't want to buy it because she's not good at painting.' How can anybody make a statement that somebody's not good at anything at age four? What a terrible message to pass on to a child. . . . I had another child who, in kindergarten, had drawn a pink giraffe. The teacher was very critical. 'A giraffe is not pink,' she said, and she told him to do it over. But he wouldn't. He never drew again, and when I saw him in therapy years later, here was this kid with tremendous artistic ability and creativity that had been killed by his failure to meet expectation in this one little area."

It's important to take the pressure off children, "to give them room without making judgments," said Fink. "The seven-year-old comes to her father and says 'I got a B on my paper. Is that terrible?' The answer is 'No, it's not terrible. In fact it's terrific. It's twice as good as a C, four times as good as a D.' And you don't say that the child will do better next time, because that builds in an expectation" and creates pressure that the child is better off without.

Unquestionably, said Fink, "praise is a helluva lot better than the opposite—contempt and punishment. We need praise to have good self-esteem, but it should be appropriate. Praise for things that are not praiseworthy builds narcissism, not self-esteem. But praise for what is terrific gives a child a great sense of competence." He hesitated a moment, and then repeated: "Reserve praise for things that are praiseworthy. . . . But there is a caveat. Early in life heavy doses of praise for everything are good, especially in toilet training. Give positive feedback for things that are right, but never mention negatives for things that are wrong. I know about a situation in which the little boy went to the toilet, then called his mother, who praised him lavishly. But that wasn't enough for the little boy, who asked his mother to keep the stool for Daddy to see when he got home from work. So the mother kept it for five or six hours until Daddy came home. Believe me, that's ultimate praise."

Nancy Samalin, who directs parent-guidance workshops and who wrote the book *Loving Your Child Is Not Enough,* agreed with Fink. Praise is much better than criticism. Frequent praise is a fine way to increase the child's cooperation with the parent, she told me. "When the child does something you like, make sure you acknowledge it. 'You took out the garbage, and I didn't have to remind you.' Or 'Your teeth are so bright, I had to put on sunglasses.' For a three-year-old that's really great."

Psychologist Philip Zimbardo, an acclaimed authority on shyness, told me that the authoritarian parent who withholds praise contributes greatly to the child's development of shyness. The authoritarian parent "is rule-bound, like a prison guard. Everything is regulated by rules; everything is highly structured. The child may learn social skills, but typically he ends up feeling inadequate or else he has low self-esteem. . . . Often there is a lot of punitiveness when the child breaks rules. Often there is verbal abuse and the use of labels: 'You dummy . . . You fat slob . . . You're so worthless that not even your grandmother could love you.' The child grows up and fears to take a risk if there's no rule to handle the situation. Then he leaves home and finds that there are not always rules, and he clings to the status quo. He never challenges the system. By definition he is shy."

The style that helps a child bloom in all ways is what Zimbardo calls "authoritative" parenting. The two words—authoritarian and authoritative—sound somewhat alike, but in meaning they are poles apart. The authoritative style "communicates unconditional love to the child. Most parents say that they love their children, but the love is given with hooks attached: 'I love you if . . . I love you if you perform in desirable ways . . . I will not love you if you hit your sister, if you don't clean your room, if you don't make the Little League team.' Parents establish an endless series of contingencies . . . or else they say 'I'll give you more love if . . .' And love becomes an economic commodity. The authoritative parent communicates: 'I love you because you exist. When you do something wrong, you will get punished, but I love you. When you do right things, you will be rewarded, but that doesn't mean that I love you more.' The result is that the child grows up feeling all right about himself, and there's no reason for shyness" or anything else that can undermine the realization of his potential.

Praise, Praise and More Praise

Educational consultant Richard P. Gallagher is the most enthusiastic advocate of praise anybody is likely to meet. When I asked him for some specific things parents can do to reinforce positive self-image in their elementary-school-age child, he summed up his feelings in three words: "Plenty of praise." He elaborates:

· Praise effort above all else, even if the result isn't something to write to Grandma about.

· Praise by words and by a hug, a smile, a hand on the shoulder—anything that suggests warmth, approval, understanding.

· Praise everything. This includes the child's friendliness, kindness, generosity, enjoyment of learning, good sportsmanship, anything at all.

· Let your child "overhear" you tell your parents and friends about his good qualities.

· Plant messages in your child's ear when the child is being tucked into bed. Ideal messages include "I'm proud of how hard you're trying in school . . . You're really a great kid . . . God blessed me with you . . . You're a good kid because you always try your best."

Gallagher said adults also need praise, but we seem to understand the importance of that and we do it. I come to see you and I say 'I like your tie' or 'I like the way your office is set up.' You think 'Gee, he's smart to recognize what I have going for me,' and you feel good about it and you flip it back to me, with a compliment in return. But parents often seem to feel that they don't have the time to do this with a child. Why? I don't know, except that maybe it mirrors how they were treated by their parents when they were children. My parents always said good things to me. As a teacher, I said good things naturally to my students. Maybe if you learn it early, you pass it on."

While it may be difficult for many parents to praise, it's often not so difficult for them to criticize their child, said Gallagher. "If you have enough time to think before you open your mouth to criticize, you might ask 'Is it really worth saying?' Most of the time it's not. Most of the time negative comments don't do much, if anything, to shape a child in positive ways."

As Gallagher said, praise works with adults, too, and Mark J. Tager makes it a point to stress the merits of praise as the head of the Chicago-based Great Performance, Inc., which designs health-promotion programs for corporations and helps executives work more effectively with employees. Tager, who has a medical degree from Duke University and who co-authored the book *Working Well*, told me that praise helps not only employees but also bosses to become better at their jobs. His advice to employees who want to help their bosses:

"Develop a relationship with the boss, a relationship that will put you in a position where you can give feedback. Bosses are like the rest of us. They often need feedback on how they're coming across. Listen to the boss and praise the boss. That's the key to developing a relationship. Try to 'catch' the boss doing something right, and then give him some good, old-fashioned, task-specific feedback. I'm not talking about earning Brownie points. I'm talking about feedback that is immediate, specific, related to the action, not general. Something like 'I was relieved to get your memo. You did an excellent job of clarifying what I should be doing this week.' If you do this long enough—listen and praise—you'll develop trust and mutual respect with the boss. These are the missing ingredients in corporate life today—trust and mutual respect."

If Some Is Good, Is a Lot Better?

Is it possible to give too much praise? I once interviewed an educator who suggested that all parents make it a point to say ten times every day to their child 'I think you're a great kid; I love you.' If parents did that, she said, children would grow up feeling good about themselves, and they'd be ready to tackle the world. Did she practice what she preached with her own child? Yes, indeed, she said. "When I started telling him, it was hard for him to accept. He said 'Great kid? Aw, come on, Mom, you're just telling me that because you're my mother.' And I said 'That's right, but you're still a great kid, and I love you.'"

What about that? A little heavy perhaps? Or on target? I asked educator Michael DeSisto if he would encourage parents to do this. His answer was no. The reason: "If you said it ten times a day, you couldn't possibly mean it. It would be automatic. There's a big difference between saying 'You're great; I love you' and feeling 'You're great; I love you.' You've got to do whatever you can do honestly—a smile, a wink, a touch, whatever. If it's real, it's appropriate, but if it's done by rote, it's dishonest—and nobody recognizes dishonesty as readily as children. If you can hug your child and really feel it, that's fine. Hug your child. If the best you can do is a smile, then smile. But let it be real. Don't follow a formula. Be honest in your feelings toward your child."

What about negative feelings? Should they be communicated, too? Absolutely, said DeSisto, if the feelings are authentic. It's appropriate to say "I hate you at this moment"—just as it's appropriate in more sunny times to say "My life is rich because of you." It's important for parents to be willing to risk honesty.

A child who gets too much praise from parents—and the only child is at high risk of too much praise—is set up for unrealistic expectations of how it will be in the outside world, said psychiatrist Alan Summers. "If you always tell your child that he's drawn a simply wonderful picture, whether it's simply wonderful or not, the child begins to feel automatically entitled to strokes from the world. When he doesn't get them, he doesn't understand why, and he feels cheated and even betrayed. His wife is supposed to find him irresistible; the boss is supposed to recognize him as a prodigy and propel him onto the fast track. When these things don't happen, and often they don't, he becomes angry. . . . He may go to great lengths to try to set up situations in which he can be a winner, and he may be very successful. His basic need is that he needs reality to conform to the idea that he is a winner."

Excessive praise that is repeated over a period of time can be bad in another way, too. It can generate an unrealistic sense of self and cause a person to become naive and in danger of being taken advantage of. Here's an example of that, from the casebook of psychiatrist Pirooz Sholevar: The female only child is constantly told by her parents that she's the core of the universe—the most beautiful, the brightest, the most desirable. She meets a man who delivers a line that most women would laugh at: "You're the core of the universe, the most beautiful, the brightest, the most desirable woman I've ever met." But *she* buys it hook, line and sinker, because it's in sync with what she believes about herself. After all, if Mommy and Daddy said it, it must be true. And she finds herself victimized in ways that would not be possible if she had a more realistic sense of herself and the world.

Praise from the Inside

If we, as only children, have a basic sense of who we are, our strengths and our limitations, we're in a position to do something very nice for ourselves. We can pat ourselves on the back, if it's appropriate, and otherwise do some self-stroking. In many of my speeches, when I'm talking about ways in which we can be good to ourselves, I suggest that we should make it a point to give ourselves at least as many strokes for our achievements as we give ourselves lashes for our shortcomings. If we don't stroke ourselves, who will? The answer is that, very likely, nobody will. We need to feel, from the inside, that we're okay.

We don't have to make a big deal out of it. Something simple will do nicely: "I really liked the way I handled that meeting." Or: "I was pleased I was able to get my point across in a way that everybody seemed to appreciate."

One of the best ways to stroke ourselves is to give ourselves permission to savor the taste of something that we have accomplished. Psychiatrist John Bulette put it this way: "If you strive toward a goal and achieve it, then, yes, you can go on toward the next goal, but in a mature way. Take the time to enjoy what you have achieved. I like what Willie Stargell of the Pirates said after the 1979 World Series when somebody asked what he was going to do next. He said, 'Man, the next thing I'm going to do is really enjoy this.' And this is very critical, enjoying the achievement. The person who moves on without savoring is missing something."

I attach so much importance to this notion of savoring our achievements because it took me a long time to be able to do it. For so many years I felt that I had to move on to the next challenge and that looking back on what I had done meant that I was standing still. How could I possibly get on with the business of succeeding unless I ran as fast as I could? It wasn't until after I came to terms with my only-child perfectionism and bigger-than-life need to achieve that I was able to ease off and sniff the flowers and squint into the sunset without worrying that I was wasting time. When you're running so fast, it's not possible to sniff or squint or do anything else that's helpful, and the tragedy is that you don't realize how much of life's sweetness is eluding you.

When There Is No Praise

What happens when an only child grows up with virtually no praise at all? The answer is obvious and brutal: He feels unloved, unworthy, unwanted—and he compensates in whatever ways he can find, perhaps by trying to be a star in everything he undertakes. Let me tell you a story that has a happy, even if tearful, ending.

They often met for late lunch on Thursdays, Paul Mitchell, a seventy-two-year-old dentist, and his daughter Mary Monica Mitchell, and as he drove into Philadelphia from his office in Trenton, New Jersey, he had no reason to suspect that something was about to happen that forever would be burned into his heart and soul. He parked his car a block from the restaurant, hurried inside, and there she was, the successful businesswoman, partner in a growing public-relations agency, the first-born of his three daughters.

They kissed lightly, and she signaled to the waiter that it was time to bring out the champagne. They sipped, smiled, carried on the banter of two people who are quietly comfortable with each other, whose intimacy has weathered the gales of two broken marriages—one for each of them.

"Dad," she said, "I have something for you. A gift. It's something I want you to have." She reached under the table and pulled out a long flat package wrapped in plain brown paper. "I didn't have time to get it wrapped with nice paper and a ribbon and everything. I just picked it up from the framer, about fifteen minutes ago."

Paul Mitchell wrinkled his forehead. "From the framer?" He broke into a broad smile. "Say, what is this?"

"Go ahead and open it." Then she leaned back to watch.

He removed the paper carefully, as if it were the most precious on earth, and then he took it out, the blue frame that held a red mat around a photograph of his daughter and some words that had been set in type, hundreds of words.

"Mary . . ."

"Read it, Dad."

Paul Mitchell pulled his eyeglasses from his jacket pocket and began to read. "Oh, God . . . Mary." At first he smiled in disbelief. Then he sobbed softly, and finally he unleashed tears that came like waves. "Oh, I can't believe you'd do this for me. Mary . . ."

"Dad, I wanted to. I love you so much."

"Mary, you can't know what this means to me . . . I'm so embarrassed, crying like this, but I can't help it."

"It's okay to cry, Dad."

He was overcome with love for his daughter.

Paul Mitchell never knew his father, who was a priest in the Byzantine Rite of the Catholic Church, which until 1941 permitted Byzantine priests in the United States to be married. His father died one month before he was born, and Paul was brought up as an only child by his mother. "I lived a gracious, cultured life, in genteel poverty," he would say. But when he was thirteen, his mother married a man who was just sixteen years older than Paul himself, and this would change the context of his life forever.

"I didn't understand it at the time, but he and I constantly vied for my mother's affection and attention. We had this rivalry, and I resented him terribly. I hated him, this man who was going to bed with my mother and taking my place in her life. My mother was cultured, from a gracious family background, and he was from a blue-collar family, a cantor in the Byzantine Rite church, which was where he met my mother. The things I took for granted, the easy grace and manners I grew up with, were things he had to learn. My mother taught him, and he was being raised by her, just like I was. It was like she had two children.

"I tried to put him in the background, to be so special, to achieve so much that my mother would notice me and push him away somewhat. But she tried to bring us together. She said 'He doesn't understand, but you can.' That's a helluva thing to say to a thirteen-year-old boy. For weeks I cried all the time. My mother made me call him Dad. If she'd put a knife in my back and twisted, she couldn't have hurt me any more than that. She didn't know what she was doing. I understand that now. She was naive. She told me: 'I married him; now you must love him.' I was enraged. 'Don't try to get me to love him. *I* didn't marry him!'

"He was a rather nice man, really. He's eighty-eight now, and we're good friends. I never had the talent he had, but I knew how to sell myself when I was a kid. He could sing opera. He had a great voice. But when we'd go somewhere to a party, everybody would ask me to sing, and I'd do some big-band songs and nobody would pay any attention to him; that really hurt him, as if his blue-collar background made it impossible for him to be a success. . . . My mother and her friends tried to make him feel comfortable, but he never seemed relaxed.

"I went to Penn, and I was captain of the lightweight football team, the 150-pound team, and I was a tough guy. I could be dying on the inside, but nobody ever knew it. I played hurt many times. I'd be bleeding and not feel anything. I remember being on the sidelines once during practice, and I heard my coach say to another coach: 'He doesn't know what it is to be hurt.' But I knew. God, how I knew. It was all on the inside, and my character development came from it. I was fierce and competitive, and there was this rage within me. I was going to prove that I was the best, at whatever I did."

Paul's mother and stepfather never came to watch him play football, because his stepfather didn't want to see him in the spotlight, and his mother was fearful she would be showing favoritism if she came to a game. It was a disappointment that never healed for Paul Mitchell. Football was, after all, the big thing in his life. It's why everybody knew him, how he became a big man on campus, how he was able to get into a fraternity and be accepted by the rich kids even though he had no money.

In his senior year, Penn played its traditional rival, Rutgers, at Franklin Field, and 14,000 people were expected. Paul got two tickets, and his mother and stepfather promised to come, just this one time, because it was so important to him. But they never arrived. "Something came up at the last minute. He pulled that kind of stuff all the time. I was absolutely devastated. I felt so rejected, so unloved. . . . That was my last game. Nobody who meant anything to me, who loved me, ever saw me play."

Mary Monica Mitchell went to a football game once with her father, and what happened prompted her to write a story. It wasn't anything special, she thought, but when she got it down on paper, all 750 words, the people who read it were excited about it, and a community newspaper editor asked for permission to print it. That surprised her. It surprised her, too, that so many people, when they read the story, choked on their emotions, cried, said things like "Mary, this is beautiful. What did your Dad think about it?" That's when she decided she would have the story set in type, get her picture taken in her father's 1938 letter sweater, and have it all framed for him in Penn's red and blue. The words for the story "just came to me," and surely they came from the heart, not the head:

I grew up believing that the University of Pennsylvania Quakers were the only football team there was. My father taught my sisters and me every Penn fight song, drinking song and, of course, "The Red and the Blue," complete with perfect hand movements. But he never taught us the game itself. He seemed to believe that Penn football was, quite simply, something one knew.

But somehow the osmosis never permeated the convent schools I attended. I ended up being my father's "artsy creative" daughter, and I was decidedly uninterested in the prospect of twenty-two young men forming very curious squatting positions, holding them perfectly balanced for a moment, and then attacking each other with consuming passion for another moment just so they could do it all over again.

My younger sisters fared better at co-ed schools. When Dad took me to Penn games, it seemed blasphemous to ask him what was going on down on the field. So it wasn't until this past fall, at the age of thirty-seven, that I got around to making this proposal: I agreed to accompany Dad to the Penn-Navy game, provided he explained the game to me, play by play.

"Dads are supposed to teach," I added testily. He countered with an invitation to the Penn-Princeton lightweight game the night before at Franklin Field. That way, he claimed, I could "hear the clash of the shoulder pads" from the sidelines, where he always watched with the lightweight coach, team, and managers. I doubt if he ever missed one of those games since the days when he played in them himself.

We agreed to meet at Franklin Field on a Friday evening. Instinct told me I was in for a memorable night. At last Dad would share "his" Penn with me. Not to be outdone, I dug into an old trunk and resurrected his football letter sweater, class of '38, that he'd long forgotten. I strode up to Franklin Field decked out in blue pants, maroon muffler, sporting his very own letter. When I was within earshot, I called "Hello." For a split second, we might have been the only people there. The shock of seeing his first-born as he once was, gangly but enthusiastic, rendered my Dad speechless, then tearful, then beaming. He proudly introduced me to everybody in sight, and he explained the game to me with care and attention.

At halftime we visited the then-deserted Varsity Club and inspected his name on the wall. For the first time he told me about Penn, about a period in his life that probably had been fuller and happier and filled with more laughter than any other. I heard about his singing solos with the Glee Club during the big-band era, about managing a fraternity, about living rich with no money. He recounted these stories as we looked out onto Franklin Field. It was just the two of us together at the Varsity Club. For him, it could have been 1938 all over again, and we were sharing it.

I laughingly asked how my fiercely protective grandmother coped with watching her only child regularly attacked by all those mean-looking young athletes. Quite suddenly, it was back to the present again, and I saw a half-century of pain etched across his face. "She never saw me play ball," he said. "No one in my family ever came."

In that instant I understood Wordsworth's meaning when he wrote of "spots of time"—apocalyptic moments frozen and preserved in order to elucidate a broader point. Here, on timeless Franklin Field, my father and I had just shared such a moment.

No one in the family ever watched you play? It's not so any more, Dad. I have.

Paul Mitchell removed his glasses, unable to read any more, sobbing quietly, fumbling for his champagne glass.

"Mary I can't tell you what this means to me."

"I love you, Dad."

— 8 —

The Spoiled Only Child: Is It Inevitable?

China has got a problem. It must feed twenty-one percent of the world's population on seven percent of the world's land that is fit for cultivation.

In an effort to control population growth, China in 1979 undertook a strict policy of one child per couple, with severe penalties imposed on couples who violate the policy. The impact of this on population won't be known fully until the end of the century, but something else is emerging right now with frightening clarity: China is producing a generation of only children who have become "little emperors," who in the Western world would be known as spoiled brats.

In 1986 the newspaper *China Youth News* published a twelve-part series entitled "The Little Suns in Our Lives" that painted some disturbing portraits.

An example: The parents of one third-grade boy bought him whatever he wanted. He dined on meat pies while his parents ate porridge. He spurned clothing that had been worn once. After his grandfather spanked him for starting a fight in school, he took a pair of scissors and threatened to kill himself until the grandfather apologized and bought him a new toy.

Another example: A seven-year-old girl's parents asked her to empty the chamber pot, but she emptied only half because, she said, she was not the only one who had used it.

Asked the newspaper: "What will be the outcome if parents allow this willfulness to continue?"

About nine percent of China's children under fourteen are only children. This amounts to 30.5 million, and they are concentrated largely in the early grades. Eight of every ten first-graders are only children, and this ratio is expected to increase over the next five years as the government tightens enforcement of the one-child policy. What is happening in China provides a glimpse into what can go wrong when parents don't know how to bring up an only child, how to set limits, when to say no, when to pull rank and lay down the law.

In reporting the problem, *The Washington Post* quoted a Chinese education official who said that many only children are so doted upon by their parents that they become timid, overbearing, lazy, self-indulgent or contemptuous of physical labor. Most only children have "weak points, such as low ability to care for themselves, selfishness, willfulness and arrogance." Another official said that only children, spoiled by their parents, tended to become "hot-tempered and pay little respect to parents and older generations."

Chinese newspapers constantly warn adults against indulging in what is known as the "4-2-1 syndrome," in which four grandparents and two parents pamper the only child. But what is a parent to do? One father, a taxi driver, told an interviewer that he had no choice but to spoil his only son. His wife worked as a store clerk, so care of their two-year-old boy was left to the child's paternal grandparents. "I don't see him very often, and he takes advantage of me." The father said that his son insisted on two pony rides a day in a park near the family's apartment. "When it is so hot, he eats Popsicles one after the other. It is making his stomach bad, but if we don't give them to him, he screams and rolls around on the floor, and it affects our neighbors."

The Chinese government, trying to convince couples of the advantages of having one child, has launched a propaganda campaign. The only child has better physical development, wider interests, a quicker mind, a keener sense of competition and greater thirst for knowledge, according to a government dispatch. And there's more: The only child also benefits from the parents' ability to afford luxuries that otherwise would be out of reach.

Chinese officials said they were confident that they would be able to resolve the only-child problem by educating parents in 20,000 "parents' schools" that have been set up across the country and by putting more emphasis on physical labor for only children. In school the children are assigned tasks, such as washing their handkerchiefs, as a way to help them learn to take care of themselves. Parents' schools urge parents to encourage their children to help prepare dinner, sweep the floor and wash dishes. Said a regional education official: "Encouraging them to work will help get rid of some of their arrogance."

But, concluded *The Washington Post*, some parents say that no amount of education or propaganda is going to change the bottom line. "I know I shouldn't give him any more soda," said a father as he watched his eighteen-month-old son happily slurp his fifth cup of orange soda. "What do you want me to do? I only have one child."

In America, Too?

Does it have to be this way? Must the only child live out his widely accepted script of being a spoiled brat? The answer, happily, is no, it doesn't have to be this way, but it's up to parents to rewrite the script. Sometimes that's difficult for parents to do because they grossly overvalue the only child. Here's a casebook example from psychiatrist Pirooz Sholevar of Jefferson Medical College:

"The father had manual jobs, three of them, one during the day, one at night and another on weekends. He was working to send his only daughter to a prestigious school, one of the most expensive in the country. At school the daughter spent money like she was a member of the jet set. Nobody ever would have guessed her father's status. But it backfired . . . the whole thing. The daughter associated with people who, when they found out about her father, looked down on him, and she became ashamed of him. It was one of the most painful experiences I ever had, as a therapist. The father sacrificed himself for her, and she walked away from him. It was heartbreaking."

Having an overvalued child is a bad deal for everybody, including the parents, because it's not possible to have an overvalued child without having an undervalued parent. The child grows up expecting everything to be given to him, without any effort on his part, while the parents, like those in China, eat porridge, and in effect lose their ability to parent because it's not possible to lead unless you're first in the pecking order.

Why would parents allow this to happen? Answer: There isn't a rational answer. It happens because parents want to be "good" to their only child.

To understand what goes on, it's necessary to understand how the only child came into being. Sholevar offered this scenario: Often the only child is conceived after many years of effort and perhaps after multiple miscarriages. When the child at last arrives, as a flesh-and-blood infant, he is viewed almost as a miracle baby by the parents, who feel honored by being given a child and convinced that an exceptional thing has happened to them. Along with this, there is a corresponding fantasy: The child can be taken away at any moment, so he must be protected . . . and cherished like no other child on earth. If two people have spent ten years trying to have a child, if it has been their life goal, then it's difficult for them to keep things in perspective. The child is the realization of their hopes, dreams, aspirations, and in some ways he can be viewed as the justification for their existence. If they lose him, they have lost their reason for living. The same feelings are shared by parents who in their late thirties adopt a child after accepting their infertility and who, because of their age and the high cost of adoption, agree that this will be their only child.

The more we invest in something, the greater is our fear of losing it. That's human nature. If you have a $150 painting in the living room, you don't worry that it's going to get away from you. But what if it's a $400,000 painting? Then you may be concerned to the point of cold sweat that somebody will break in and steal it or that your house will burn down. Every time you hear about a fire, your worries are activated. It's the same with some parents of only children. They overvalue and overprotect, and in a way they live their lives to serve the child. It's almost a slavery phenomenon, and it inverts the balance of power.

In a conventional family, parents know what is best for the child, and they try to do what is best, even when it's unpopular. Parents are always the boss, always one-up on the child. But parents of an overvalued child, instead of being in charge, can find themselves serving the child. They're often in a one-down position, and the only child calls the shots. Parents may try to compete with each other to get the child to say "I love you more." In effect, parents bid for the child's attention, almost as if an auction is going on, and the child goes to the highest bidder. The outcome of this can be forecast without much reservation: a child who is spoiled rotten.

When There's Too Much Self-Love

The foundation that supports the only child's spoiled nature is excessive narcissism, self-love out of control, always putting himself first even if it means trampling on other people.

There are lots of funny stories about narcissism, and Leo Madow, former chairman of psychiatry at the Medical College of Pennsylvania, knows most of them. Here's one:

> Two little boys confronted each other, and one said: "I went to a party last night."
> The other responded: "No, you didn't."
> "What do you mean? Of course, I went to a party."
> "It's impossible that you could have been at a party; I wasn't there."

Madow, who wrote a book entitled *Love* and devoted many pages to narcissism, said that the story illustrates a classic example of somebody who feels that nothing goes on except in his world. There are many only children who have this feeling and whose parents have done nothing to make them face the cold light of reality. Here is another Madow story:

> The mother gets a note from the teacher that says her son, Johnny, is misbehaving. Would she please come in for a conference at her earliest convenience?
> So the mother meets the teacher, who says Johnny's problem is that he talks in class when he's supposed to be listening.
> The mother thinks for a moment and then advises the

teacher: "Hit the kid in front of him, and Johnny will get the idea."

All too often the only child gets too much of a good thing, said Madow. Every child starts out feeling at the center of the universe—that's an essential ingredient in growing up in a healthy way. But for the healthy growth to continue, the child at some early point has to begin to learn more about his limits, about where he ends and where the rest of the world begins. The clearer the child is on that, the more emotionally mature he is. The only child's handicap is that he is, unfortunately, at the center of the family constellation. In addition he may be the only grandchild or perhaps the first grandchild, and this reinforces the idea that he's number one. This is a barrier to the only child's efforts to accept limitations in the real world, and the child may carry unrealistic expectations for far too long and expect far too much. To illustrate this, another Madow story:

> The only child, who was ten, always was complaining and wanting more, and so the mother decided that she was going to saturate him, give him anything and everything for one whole day.
>
> He got up when he wanted to and immediately asked for doughnuts. The mother made doughnuts. Then she went with him on the itinerary that he had drawn, first to the zoo, then to the playground and then to the park. After that they went to a double-feature movie and then they had hamburgers and double malts.
>
> At last they came home, and he watched TV until 10:30. The mother was exhausted. "OK, Jerry, it's time to go to bed."
>
> "I want to watch more TV."
>
> "Look, you've had everything you wanted today, but now it's 10:30 and it's bedtime."
>
> Jerry's face twisted in disbelief. "See, you never give me anything."

This, said Madow, is the kind of narcissistic dissatisfaction that can be seen in only children who are put at the center of the universe and never made to confront limits. If they aren't helped to change, they are handicapped as adults. "Is narcissism necessary? Should we try to train it out of children? The answer clearly is that, yes, it is necessary, in proper amounts, and, no, we shouldn't try to train it out because we all must have a sense of our own value. We get into trouble with narcissism when there's too much, and there's too much when, if you don't get what you want, you go into a depression or a rage. There's too much when you constantly overreact, when narcissistic injury cripples you, when you have a temper tantrum because you were excluded from something. . . . If you're the center of the universe and if nobody teaches you anything about limits, you're going to be furious if anybody tries to take away from you anything that you want."

Madow said he has encountered many excessively narcissistic only children who had a constant battle with weight. "If they don't get what they want, they become frustrated, and their answer is to eat, to give themselves some satisfaction." Only children who are adopted may be especially prone to narcissistic pain, he said. "No matter what the parents who adopted the child do, it's hard for the child to overcome the reality that he was given away. He was rejected. Any way you slice it, he was given away by his mother, and the child is stuck with the fact that he was given away. Maybe the biological mother wanted him to have better things, but she still gave him away. If the adoptive mother crosses the child, he may say something like 'See, you don't love me, just like my mom.' The adoptive mother can kill herself trying to prove her love to him, but she can't succeed."

In therapy the only child can be especially difficult to treat, said Madow. "You take a child who was the apple of the parents' eye, who got everything he wanted, and then he comes into treatment, and he expects the same thing—to be the apple of the therapist's eye. The therapist has to frustrate him, and the only child doesn't like that. He may get furious, and if he can't accept the frustration and the fact that he's not going to be treated in a special way, he may quit therapy." Whether a frustrated only child continues in therapy is determined to a considerable extent by how much he was indulged by parents, by how far his worldview is warped and unreal. "If it's to powerful excess, the only child may be untreatable in regular psychotherapy. . . . Some of them never give up wanting to be treated as special. Because they once had it all, and liked it very much, they want to keep on getting it" even though the world may be turning away from them in disgust.

When the Spoiled Only Child Is an Adult

Madow said it's not uncommon for only children to remain spoiled as adults—and in many ways to continue to act like children. "You find somebody who isn't invited to a party goes into an absolute rage . . . or you take a person who isn't able to work for two days after the boss makes critical comments. One of the most painful emotional experiences is narcissistic injury," a personal hurt in which we have been wounded by something, real or imagined, that somebody else has done to us.

"I once had in therapy a man who was late for his session one day because a coal truck had parked in his driveway to unload, and he couldn't get his car out. He kept repeating 'How could they do that to me?' That was the essence of our hour. I tried to explain that *they* didn't *do* it to *him*. It could happen to anybody. They had to unload the coal . . . but he was really hurt. Man, that's narcissistic injury," and the only child is especially at risk because he has become so accustomed to having things his way.

How does a therapist deal with adult only children whose narcissism is bigger than life? Madow said that many of them open themselves to the process of being helped after they discover that extreme narcissism doesn't work. "It's not functional. The person runs into trouble and suffers, and that's why he comes to the doctor." In therapy Madow attempts to build up a working alliance and then confronts the person with evidence of what his narcissism is doing to him. Confrontation could boil down to this: "Look at what you're doing. You sound as if the world revolves around you. You're hurt when you're not invited to a party. You go into a tailspin if the boss is critical of your work. Aren't you getting enough of this? Aren't you making too much of what goes on between you and others?"

It's important for the person to be allowed to explain his feelings and emotions, to express his narcissistic rage and eventually to understand that his feelings are out of proportion to what the situation calls for. The light appears at the end of the narcissistic tunnel when the person grasps this and responds with "Aha . . . now I see." This happens so routinely in successful therapy that it has been described as the Aha phase.

Who Is That Person, Anyway?

It is the opinion of psychiatrist Sholevar that only children tend to be handicapped in a special way because they lack the ability to look at themselves realistically. "To look at yourself, you need others to look objectively at you. This quality usually comes at age ten or twelve, being able to sit outside yourself and look. Having siblings helps a lot. They're not there to build you up or tear you down. They give you an objective appraisal, but this is something that the only child doesn't get enough of, if any at all. The only child doesn't get enough experience with neutral feedback because the parents, with whom he spends so much time, are so adoring. And so the only child often is deprived of this ability of self-observation" and grows up without a realistic sense of self.

Here's a case that Sholevar remembers well:

"She was thirteen when I first saw her, the only child of parents who tried for years to get pregnant. She primarily saw herself as a superior being, because that's how her parents saw her, and she expected others to be there to admire her. If they didn't admire her, she took it as criticism. She was in treatment because she felt that nobody liked her, even though in reality she was reasonably well liked. . . . If a friend of hers played with a third friend, she felt rejected. If she was in a crowd of five friends and two of them talked between themselves, she felt excluded and unliked. She had to be the center of attention, and she expected others to fight for the privilege of being closer to her because, at home, her parents always were close to her. . . . She tried to maneuver social situations so she could snatch kids away from others, and they began to see her as an evil person, trying to steal people away, almost like a body snatcher."

Age thirteen is a time when all of us tend to want attention, said Sholevar, and it's a common time for trouble. "When only children are excluded, it can be like the sky has fallen. They can get very upset and cry all night . . . and parents pick up the pattern, and they cry all night, too. If you have five children in the family and one cries all night, the mood of the family doesn't necessarily change. It's only one of five who's crying. But if you have only one . . ."

Some other comments on being overvalued and spoiled come from psychiatrist Richard Moscotti: "Maybe parents can give the only child ten or fifteen percent more love and attention than would be normal. Maybe that's the best they can do realistically, because they've waited years to have the child, and in their eyes he's a megastar. . . . Too much love does a disservice to the child. It's like overwatering a plant. Parents can overlove and overpleasure a child, and this can be as negative as underloving."

Child psychiatrist Selma Kramer: "Only children never have to share, and they don't know how to share easily. They go way past the typical two-year-old behavior of saying 'This is mine, and you can't use it.' When you have a younger sibling who grabs for your stuff, it makes you aware that the world expects you to share. Only children don't have this, and often they're so excessively gratified that they don't develop an ordinary tolerance for frustration. Nobody ever says 'No, you can't have it because it's somebody else's turn.'"

Psychologist Carol Gantman, whose only child, Benjamin, is three and a half: "He clearly gets more undivided attention than he would if I had other children. He says 'Mommy, look,' and I have the luxury to look and spend ten minutes. He wouldn't get that if there were other children. I can see how he's developing a demandingness. 'Mommy, look at me!' And he keeps it up until I look. I asked my pediatrician how to teach him to be less demanding, and he said 'Have another kid.'"

An attorney who is an only child: "We didn't have much to share at our house when I was little, but there's no question that the only child tends to be spoiled. I think maybe parents feel guilty about not providing the only child with a playmate, and they may overcompensate by giving more to the only child. . . . What the only child gets, in capital letters, is UNDIVIDED ATTENTION. I still expect it because I always got it from my parents. I don't want anybody to look the other way when I'm talking. If they look away, I'll ask them 'OK, tell me what I said.' That's crazy because you can't expect people to pay attention to you the way your parents did, but that's the way I am. I don't think only children readily give up expecting undivided attention."

So What Can Parents Do?

If there's something that I've discovered over the years, it's that I can find interesting things going on in the least likely places. Let me tell you a story that bears directly on how parents can teach children about limits.

I was at the beach. Twice within fifteen minutes, in family groups sprawled out close enough to me so that I could hear every word, I was treated to textbook examples of effective parenting.

In one situation, the father was explaining to Charlie, who looked to be about eight, that it was lunchtime and that the choice, in the picnic basket, was between a cheese sandwich and a peanut butter sandwich. Charlie didn't like the options, and he made his feelings known: "Cheese or peanut butter? Yuck! I want roast beef." It's something that a "little emperor" might say, but the father wasn't buying it. He looked Charlie straight in the eye and, with what seemed to me a healthy amount of vigor, said: "Look, I'm telling you what I got. It's that or nothing." Charlie climbed down off the throne and announced that a peanut butter sandwich would be just fine.

The other situation involved a boy who looked old enough to know better, perhaps fourteen, who wore baggy, knee-length surfer shorts and a T-shirt that promoted a long-ago rock concert. He asked his father for five dollars so he could play some video games. At first the father seemed to pretend not to hear, but the boy persisted. "Dad, where's your wallet? I want five dollars." Finally, Dad let his son know that he had heard him. "I don't have my wallet here, and even if I did, I wouldn't give you five dollars." The boy whined. "Why not, Dad? Just five dollars. Please. Aw, c'mon."

The father made his position perfectly clear. "Look, Kevin, if you've already spent your allowance, that's your problem. Since we've been here, you've gotten to do a lot of things you wanted. We took you to Ocean City. You rode the rides. You got a T-shirt. You got a pizza. You got a surfboard. You went to the movies. I think you've had quite a lot."

"Aw, Dad, please."

"Kevin, by God, the answer is no. If you don't think you're being treated fairly, then I suggest you go to your room and think about it some more. I don't want to hear any more."

"Aw, Dad . . ."

"This discussion is finished. I'll see you at dinner—unless you keep on complaining, in which case I won't see you at dinner, because you won't be there."

Head down, Kevin trudged off, kicking sand, but, I thought, the recipient of something far more valuable than five dollars to play video games.

Why was I so pleased by what I heard in those two instances? I thought the father in the first example made clear to his son what I consider a cardinal rule of parenting: Let your child know what's available and give the child a choice. "Look, I'm telling you what I got." It's a statement with which no child can argue reasonably, at least not for very long. In the second example, the father was refreshing his son's memory about how generously he had been treated and drawing a line beyond which he should not push. That's limit-setting at its finest, and children can learn from it, even little emperors. They may kick the sand, figuratively or even literally, but *not* getting everything they want is part of growing up. An essential part.

One More Story

They had been married for nine years, a professional couple in their thirties, when they decided to have a child. Like everything else in their lives, the decision was well-thought-out.

"We began to look at our families and at how much we love our families. We always thought of ourselves in the context of being part of the family, and we really liked that. As we saw our parents getting older, with little illnesses setting in, we began to lose the sense of family forever, and that was frightening. Perhaps we could be happy for fifteen or twenty years without a child, but what would it be like when we got older? We know that we'd still like to be part of a family unit, and to do that we'd either have to produce a family or rely on nephews, nieces and friends. This clinched it for us."

The pregnancy was in the seventh month when I talked with them. They said that, after the birth, they expected their lives to be fuller.

"Our day won't end at 11:30 anymore or begin at a civilized 7:00. We won't relate to our child or to each other much differently than we do now. We'll not be different people but the same people doing different things. The content of our lives will change. We have new things to learn. But the process of how we solve problems, make decisions and relate to each other will not change. . . . People will disagree and say 'Just you wait,' but we don't believe that a child changes people."

That's what they said before their daughter arrived. I talked with them again about a year and a half later, and they said that they didn't expect to have any more children. "This is no reflection on our daughter," said the father, who is a psychologist. "We never looked at children as coming in pairs. This feels right for us, although some assume that if you have one, you'll have two. . . . There is no evidence that an only child has any special problems."

Their lives still included a busy social schedule, and, unlike some parents, they had not felt that they must be relatively homebound because of the baby. "We're fortunate that we can afford to have people help us out so we can have a social life as full as we want. We have no family around here to call on to babysit. For us to get help, we have to pay for it. We have to plan things. I can't think of a time when we turned down an invitation because of the child. It requires some juggling, but . . ."

No, they agreed, this didn't mean that they ignored their baby. What it meant was that they had kept their perspective and guarded against their role of parents becoming their basic identity. Said the father: "We're talking to you about the baby right now because you're asking about the baby. But if we were just having lunch, we wouldn't sit and talk your ear off about our child. If you asked 'How's Emily?' we'd give you a couple of sentences, and that would be it. People don't want to know the whole developmental process."

In the beginning they had the short nights that all new parents have. Said she: "We laughed a lot about it. 'Can you believe how much we're up?' We tried to keep our humor about the lack of sleep. Said he: "We knew it would end. Eventually she would sleep through the night. There are no adults who have to eat that many times a night. We worked together, as a team, even though she was breast-feeding. I'd get up, change the diaper and bring her in and my wife would feed her. Then I'd take her back. I remember thinking then 'I can't imagine how women do all of this by themselves. They're nuts not to demand that the husband participate.' I also can't imagine how a husband could let his wife do this all alone. He'd be nuts not to participate. I really got a kick out of it. . . . But many men are exposed to the viewpoint that to do this is not masculine. I think that this kind of attitude cheats them, cheats their wives, cheats their children. We didn't enjoy getting up, but it was part of the process."

They had found it necessary at times to be firm with their daughter, even though it sometimes tore at their insides. "The book said that at some point, when we put her in the crib at night, she'd cry for thirty minutes if we left her alone. Then she'd cry for fifteen minutes the second night, and on the third night she'd go right to sleep. The first night was horrible, and we asked 'How can we do this to her?' But by the third night she went right to sleep, just like the book said. Periodically she tests us and reminds us that she'd like to have it her way. We remind her that we'd like to have it our way."

Their relationship with each other, as they predicted, was "unchanged in terms of how we deal with each other. But we've added a significant subject to deal with. This means that we have less time with each other about issues between us. We have to work hard to get back to these . . . and not to focus 100 percent on the baby." He reads much less than he used to. "A few times I've not known about what was seen as a major news story. Somebody would comment and I'd say 'Gee, I haven't read about that.' I felt kind of stupid, but I realized that my priorities were elsewhere."

As we talked, the three of us, it occurred anew to me that their approach to parenting was a ringing endorsement for maturity, for waiting to have a child until the time was right, until a child was really wanted, not because it was the thing to do or because parents applied pressure to become grandparents. They were parenting in a fashion that made them happy and that surely put their only child in line to be happy, well adjusted and unspoiled.

Some Final Words

What is the best game plan that parents can adopt to heighten chances that their only child won't be overvalued, spoiled, a little emperor?

Therapists are in broad agreement here, and their thinking comes down to this: Parents must be aware of the exceptional value that they potentially may place on the only child, and they must guard against excessively gratifying the child. That's where being spoiled comes from—being gratified too much and not being frustrated enough. This is how children grow into responsible adults, by being subjected to frustration as well as gratification. This is how children learn limits and understand that the world extends beyond them.

Parents should keep their priorities straight. Their relationship comes first, and the child comes second. That's the healthy order, for everybody. A serious problem in families with an only child is that the child too often is put first and, as a result, is deprived of the valuable experience of being the odd person out. It's valuable because it promotes the notion that there are other people in life besides him, that other people can do things without him, that eventually somebody can throw a party and not invite him. Parents need to have a relationship that at times excludes the only child.

Parents can help the only child by making a special effort to invite other children about the same age from the neighborhood into the home to create a kind of sibling situation. It's in the interaction with other children that the only child can get some practical experience in sharing.

Imagine this situation: The only child has a new computer game, which he plays for hours at a time. Two friends are invited in, and they immediately want to play the game. The only child is adamant: "It's my machine. You can play when I'm finished in a couple of hours." The parents, watching the exchange, wisely intervene. "Look, there's one computer and three of you. You have to take turns." The only child steps aside, grudgingly at first, unaccustomed to not being gratified. Then he notices there's another child sitting out, too, and it occurs to him that sometimes you're in and sometimes you're out. It can be as much fun sometimes to be out as in, and it's possible to learn while you're out. It's an idealized situation, certainly, and it may not always work out this way, but it's something for parents to hold up as a model.

What about narcissism? What can parents do to help the only child acquire reasonable self-love without becoming a narcissistic neurotic? The answer is for parents to have enough love for the child so that they are able to bite the bullet and impose sometimes unpopular limits. This gives the child a good shot at narcissistic balance because he learns early that he is lovable but also that he is not the only person who has rights. One of the manifestations of love has to be the feeling by parents that they can set effective limits. Children must have limits or they can't grow up well. Unfortunately, some people continue to believe and preach that parents never should frustrate the child. But the exact opposite is true. If parents don't frustrate the child, he never gets bottle-trained, toilet-trained or anything else. Parents must be comfortable enough in their love so they can frustrate the child when it is appropriate.

9

When Love Isn't There

Psychologist Maurice Prout was saying that the only child "gets the whole pie" because there are no brothers and sisters around to dilute the intensity of the relationship with the parents. The pie, in Prout's words, "may be fresh and delicious or loaded with botulism, the best and worst of both worlds. If it's a nurturing family, with two parents who give you loads of time, who encourage a sense of attainment, then you can go for the moon, become the best you can be. If you come from poisoned parents, you may work hard to get out and strive for success as a way to escape. So two only children can end up at the same point of success even though they came from two different motivational directions."

There are many examples of only children whose drive to succeed was fueled negatively. Psychologist Judith Coche recalled one client who was "an extremely high achiever. He seemed well socialized, and he was very successful in all areas of his life—business, athletics, music. He had made a lot of money . . . but underneath all of this was this tremendous sense of emptiness. He grew up in a family with one alcoholic parent and one parent who was heavily dependent on alcohol. The parenting was so poor . . . and he got a sense very early that he would have to battle the world to survive. He could depend on his parents for nothing. He had nobody to turn to, and so he became self-sufficient," a super-achiever who was cheered by everybody. But he was so lonely that at times he felt he couldn't go on. Behind the achievement, which was a facade, there was only pain.

Consultant Edward Kuljian has worked with many "successful" people who came from troubled families. "You take a guy with a tough upbringing. His parents separated. There was little warmth when he was growing up, and he learned to live by his wits. He became wary, intense, and his philosophy was 'In this world you have only yourself.' He feels that he must beat the other guy to the punch, and he becomes a street fighter. This is a classic profile of a workaholic."

An only-child psychiatrist who said that he was speaking from personal experience explained what happens when the only child gets not enough praise and too much critical comment from parents: "You draw a circle around the home, and this is the entire universe for the kid. Within that universe, because of the criticism, he finds that he is not good enough. Later he broadens the universe, but his frame of reference stays the same—he's not good enough—and he selects data to conform to that. . . . A teacher says 'Johnny, that's a nice story you wrote and maybe next time we'll read it in class.' What Johnny hears is that the story is not good enough to read in class this time . . . and he develops a mind-set of what reality is. He knows that he's not good enough, and reality reinforces it. He can't accept a compliment. To him a compliment is like gibberish, a foreign language. It doesn't compute, and he's uncomfortable with it. 'Oh, it's nothing.' That's the best he can do because there's no reference for it in his reality. . . . He gravitates to relationships that reinforce the negatives, because that's what he knows how to handle, and he develops a certain comfort level. He may marry somebody who'll create that environment."

Psychiatrist Martin Goldberg said that when parents "have major-league craziness—incest, depression, alcoholism—the only child has got a special problem. If there are two or three siblings, he can get some support. The siblings can say 'You're not crazy. Mom and Dad are crazy.' But if you're the only child, you presume that your parents are OK and that you're crazy. There's nobody to validate you. . . . I see in therapy a lot of only children who need validation. 'Yeah, you're OK, but you're in a crazy situation.'" Goldberg said that incestuous behavior is more common in only-child families, and the reason is fairly obvious: There are more opportunities, with less possibility of being interrupted and caught. "In my experience father-daughter incest is surprisingly common. Mother-son incest is uncommon, but in the few instances I've seen, it has been between mother and only son, when the father was absent."

The Story of Melissa

She is thirty-four, strikingly good looking, with short dark hair and the long legs of a distance runner, which she is—on those rare weekends when she isn't working or flying off fifteen hundred miles to a Monday meeting. On average, she works seventy to eighty hours a week, plus what she describes as "think time," when she sits, stares into space and plans her next moves.

In her consulting business, which employs a dozen people, she is the hands-on leader, so quick-witted that she's always steps or even days ahead of everybody else. This year she expects her business to gross more than $4 million. She has a house in the country, a condominium in the city, a cottage at the seashore, a foreign-built sports car for fun, an American-made sedan for work. She's thinking about buying a boat, mostly for entertaining clients, but her accountant has been dragging his feet and asking things like "When is enough enough?"

Melissa doesn't know the answer to that question, and, although she's been in therapy off and on for almost ten years, she's not certain that she'll ever find the answer. What she is certain of is that she must achieve, build a bigger and bigger reputation, earn more and more money and erect a wall that she hopes forever will shield her from the pain of her early years, pain that cannot be eased more than temporarily by alcohol, drugs or even by love. She has been married and divorced twice, and she doubts that she ever will marry again, although she accepts dates sometimes and has been proposed to by four men who are bowled over by her physical and intellectual presence.

To understand Melissa's story, you must go back to the very beginning. Her mother was an unmarried woman who had had an affair with a married man and who, for reasons that were more social than financial, immediately put her up for adoption. When Melissa was three months old, she was adopted by a husband and wife who were nearing middle age, who were educated and prosperous and who appeared, on the surface, to be kind, gentle and caring. But appearances can be deceiving. The man often was out of town on business and, even when he was present physically, he seemed to Melissa to be absent emotionally. The mother, unfortunately for Melissa, was ever-present.

The sexual abuse began when she was four years old and continued, on a regular basis, until she was nine, when she was old enough and strong enough to get away. "She'd come into my room at night, wake me up and tell me that she couldn't sleep and would it be all right if she got in bed with me. And she would work up to it, and then she'd do it. I knew it was wrong, even as a little kid, but the thing was that it felt good, and when you're a little kid and it feels good and your mother's doing it, what are you going to do? I felt guilty as hell, like it was my fault. I felt awful most of the time." Before she was twelve, Melissa had run away from home five times.

The experience left Melissa with scar tissue that is thick and ugly. She clenched her fists and screamed: "I had sex with my mother! My very own mother! If I can't trust my mother, who can I trust? I'm afraid to trust anybody . . . and so I can't get close to anybody. How can you be married if you can't trust and can't get close?" She gulped down what remained of a vodka and tonic and bristled with rage. "How could she do this to me? Why wouldn't my father listen to me when I tried to tell him about it? Goddammit anyway, why did I have to be the one?"

The Story of Mitchell

He was twenty-seven when I first met him, serving ten to twenty years in prison for a second conviction on burglary charges. Mitchell was average in height, but that was the only thing about him that was average. He was muscular, like somebody who could compete and win in a body-beautiful contest. He was bright, an avid reader who spent hours in the prison library and who could recite poetry and argue intelligently the contemporary issues in politics. He was exceedingly good at what he did for a living, which was breaking into supermarkets. The warden described him to me as "about the best I ever saw. He could get into places that nobody else got into, and he could get out, most of the time."

Because he was a model prisoner in all ways, Mitchell was given extraordinary privileges, such as the use of a telephone in the library. Sometimes he would call me at home, in the months after I had interviewed him for a story, and we had become, in some fashion, friends. I'd answer the phone, and his greeting always would be the same: "This is the Jailbird speaking."

At first he didn't talk much about his early life, but as our relationship became more comfortable, he responded to my questions and his story unfolded. He had grown up in the rural South, as the only child of parents who had come from families that were emotionally and financially deprived, and from his earliest memories he recalled physical abuse. "I'd break a toy, and that would enrage my father, and he'd take a stick and beat me across the back and legs. I wouldn't get to the dinner table fast enough to suit my mother, and she'd slap me in the face. Like the books I now read all say, I accepted the blame. It was my fault. If I were a better boy, this wouldn't happen. But no matter what I did, how hard I tried, it didn't change anything. They still beat me and called me names. Once, when I was still really young, before my teens, I asked my father why he hit me so much, and he said that he wanted me to be tough enough to get along in the world, that the world was a place in which people got beat up all the time, that I had to be tough and that, by God, one day I would be tough enough to beat him and then I'd be ready to face the world."

I couldn't believe what I was hearing, but years later, when I listened to the words of the Johnny Cash song "A Boy Named Sue," it occurred to me that something similar to this must have been what Mitchell's parents had in mind. They were preparing him for their reality—a world that was a treacherous place in which you had to sock it to other people before they socked it to you, a world in which the glass always was half-empty, never half-full. It was an incredible realization for me. I never thought such things happened, except in fiction.

Mitchell had pounded his father into the red clay at age seventeen, and he was off to see the world, first in the Navy, where his service was undistinguished, and then in a series of menial jobs that provided him with beer money but not much more. His expressed need for money eventually brought him into contact with an older man who had served time in prison and who taught Mitchell the tricks of breaking and entering. Mitchell was an apt pupil, and before long he was on his own, coming down through ceilings in ways that Batman never would have attempted. He stole a lot of money before he was caught the first time and put on probation. He stole a lot more money before he was caught the second time, which was when I got to know him.

What would he do when he got out of prison? Mitchell had a wife and a son somewhere in the Midwest and he was going to look for them. They would be a happy family. He seemed so certain of it. Because of his exemplary behavior, Mitchell was released early and I lost track of him—until one morning when I noticed a one-paragraph item buried deep inside the newspaper, at the bottom of a page. It said that he had been arrested while breaking into a supermarket—through the roof, naturally. I cried.

A Voice on the Telephone

I had written a newspaper column on my perceptions of what it means these days to be a man, and I indicated that the light at the end of the tunnel was being provided by the young men who, unlike some of us in middle age, recognized that sensitivity and openness and not brute strength and the strong silent approach were what genuine masculinity was all about. I wrote that many of today's young men had grown up with the philosophy that it's okay to practice the violin instead of playing baseball, that it's prudent and not cowardly to stay out of the tallest tree, that it's appropriate to cry when you're hurting, that it's more damaging to fulfill an outrageous definition of manhood than to throw a baseball like a girl.

On the day that the column was printed, my most unusual telephone call came not from a man who wanted to debate maleness but from a woman who wanted . . . well, at first I wasn't sure what she wanted. All I knew was that she sounded terribly drunk.

"Yes, I've been drinking all day," she said, "ever since I read that damn column of yours."

I asked why she was so upset.

"You wrote about little boys who climb trees and play baseball with their fathers. Do you know how close fathers are to their sons? Do you know how many things they do together? Do you know how wonderful it is to be loved by a father? Do you know . . . no, dammit, there's no way you could know. Nobody knows. That's why I'm drunk."

Normally, I don't pursue conversations with drunks, but this time it was different, perhaps because the voice, even through the haze of intoxication, carried a strong suggestion of many years of formal education and many years of unspeakable pain, too. I asked why she was drinking.

"My father wanted a son, and when he got me instead, as his only child, he was so disappointed. Do you know what that's like—to know, even as a kid, that your father is disappointed not because of anything you've done but because of what you are? All my life I've wanted only one thing: to please my father, to make him happy, to get him to tell me that he loved me."

She was beginning to sob, but she kept talking. "When I was about ten, I climbed the highest tree in the neighborhood, and I shouted 'Look, Daddy! I can do anything a boy can do!' I tried to learn to throw a baseball like a boy. 'Look, Daddy! See how far I can throw!' But he never looked, dammit. He never looked, no matter what I did. And he never loved me, not like he'd have loved a son."

Much of her adult life had been devoted to chasing the same impossible dream, she said. She had been graduated at the head of her college class, and she had thrown herself into her career and had been more successful than most men. She knew that in so many ways she still was crying "Look, Daddy!" but the result always was the same. Daddy never showed that he was pleased or that she was loved. How could he? After all, she was a girl, and Daddy had wanted a boy. Sometimes, if she drank enough, the pain seemed to go away for a little while, and it was with that expectation that she had uncorked the bottle on this very day after reading my column about little boys and tall trees and baseballs.

"It hurts so much," she said, "to know that you don't matter and that you'll never matter. But you wouldn't understand that, would you?"

I ended the conversation by hanging up the telephone when her language became abusive. But I did understand the tortured life that she had described, because many other people, over the years, had told me substantially the same story.

There was the man who sought relief not from the bottle but through primal therapy, who had pounded his fists against a wall and screamed "Daddy, I hate you! Do you hear me, Daddy? I hate you because of what you've done to me!"

There was the woman who had confronted an empty chair in a therapist's office and said in a businesslike voice "Mother, all my life I've tried to make you proud of me, but I'm not going to try any more. I'm learning how to be proud of myself. I still love you, Mother, but I don't need your approval any more."

And on and on it went that afternoon, as the telephone call from the woman whose father wanted a boy pried loose memories of past interviews with people, many of them only children, who had struggled, with varying degrees of success, to come to terms with parental displeasure and with their own attempts to resolve it. Is there anything in the world stronger than our need to have our parents approve of us and love us?

No, probably not. Psychologist Philip Bobrove described this yearning as "a universal condition. We all seek it." But the irony of it is that this endless search for parental favor is "a doomed enterprise. We cannot please our parents because in most cases they're not aware of what they're asking" from their children, the perfection that they themselves never reached. Even as adults, when we try intellectually to approach this legacy from childhood, we often are not successful because "we're not adults trying to please adults but still little only children trying to please a mystic force."

There are hundreds of different kinds of therapy that purport to teach us ways to deal with all of this, but no one therapy works for everybody, said Bobrove. The bottom line in most therapies tends to be forgiveness. "Most of us come from imperfect parents, and we have no choice but to forgive. If we can't forgive our parents for what they did to us, what can we expect from our own children?"

At that instant I wished that I had asked the intoxicated woman on the telephone if she had any children. Perhaps, I thought, somewhere out there was her own son or daughter crying in anguish "Look, Mommy!"

"Like A Horse at a Rodeo"

Her name is Anne, and she has a four-year-old son. From the very beginning of her marriage and even before—when she and the man who would become her husband lived together—there existed what she described as "heavy physical abuse." She was, in her words, "scared stiff to leave. I was afraid he'd come after me and beat me silly. Why did I go ahead and marry him? That's what everybody asks. The answer is I felt I was going to be his salvation. I was going to love him and save him."

It was, she would say, a fool's game that she played. "I kept thinking that if I changed, maybe things would be better." For a while, after the baby was born, it appeared that things had become better, at least better than before. The physical abuse tapered off and "maybe I'd get slapped only once every three or four weeks." But the psychological abuse continued without letup, and often her husband would say: "You lost your shape when you had the baby . . . You're fat . . . You don't know how to wear your makeup right . . . You're stupid . . . The only way you're able to keep your job is that the people who work with you don't know how incompetent you are . . . Take a look at the young girls out there and then look at yourself, look at what you've become . . . You're a pig."

She knew it wasn't true, Anne would say, but the strange thing was that "you begin to believe anything if you hear it often enough." Then the beatings resumed, on her and the boy, too. "He hit me on the forehead with his fist, not all that bad, but I went to the doctor. Then the next week he hit me on the arm, which turned black and blue. I went to see the doctor again, and he said 'Look, you know where to find the police, don't you?' I began to realize that real people don't live like this," and for the first time she began to consider her options. No, she really didn't have to put up with this anymore and she wouldn't—if he ever abused her again.

One day she came home early, and her husband was there. He grabbed her by the hair and pulled her face close to his. She looked straight into his rage-swollen eyes and nearly was blinded by what she saw. "Oh, my God, this man is insane!" The next day she packed some clothing, and she and her son left and moved into a shelter for abused women and their children.

I met Anne there a few weeks after her arrival. She said her only child, Jason, bears the scars of what happened, scars that are perhaps even deeper than her own. "He has a great many problems. . . . He has accepted the role of his father, and I now have a miniature husband living with me. I don't allow him to beat on me, but he comes at me full speed ahead, like a horse at a rodeo when they open the gate. When I tell him it's bedtime or bath time, he comes at me with every ounce of energy he has."

Without intervention, Jason surely is on his way to becoming a full-fledged abuser himself. Psychiatrist Loren Crabtree said abused children often grow up feeling that they deserved the treatment, and "because the way we were loved is the way we love" these children, when they become parents, not infrequently abuse their own children in turn.

The Syndrome

There are only children—and others, too—who never recover from being neglected and deprived of love and attention during the critical early months and years of their lives. Forever, they try to compensate for their loss, but they fight an uphill battle that many of them are destined to lose.

Who are these people? Take a good look, because some of them could be your friends and neighbors. By the world's standards, they are successful. Bright and hard-working, they earn big money, live in grand style and hold positions of honor and trust in their communities. Others admire them and their seemingly flawless relationships with their families. Often they are held up as models to be followed by all who desire to join the circle of life's winners.

But what others don't know is that some of these people—and nobody can determine how many—are reeling in their boots, scarred victims of what psychologist Burton Zahler calls "The Syndrome." These are people who are depressed and maybe suicidal, but what stamps them as different from others is that "they've felt this way as long as they can remember. There was no time when it started—no time that they're aware of. You get them to talk about childhood things, and they say that the feeling was there then, too."

What those who experience The Syndrome have in common, apart from depression along with their material success, is that their mothers habitually were angry or depressed when the babies were between the crucial ages of nine and nineteen months, although the mothers may have provided good physical care. That, said Zahler, is the root of the problem, which is attacked through regressive therapy in which clients go back to their beginnings and re-experience their feelings of rejection and abandonment.

As babies, said Zahler, they needed emotional support and nurturing from their mothers as they began to explore the world and assert their individuality. When they didn't get it, they developed in a way not unlike a constantly windblown tree, which produces branches only on the side away from the prevailing wind. The tree survives, but at the cost of a less efficient metabolism, since there aren't as many leaves to nourish its growth. "These children develop a similar survival adaptation. They manage somehow to become less sensitive to the suppressed negative feelings of the mother, thereby reducing their own anxiety to a manageable level . . . but one might also describe them as stunted, gnarled and lopsided in their emotional development."

As adults, they strive mightily for career success, a benchmark of only children, as a futile way to counteract their bad feelings. But, of course, no amount of success ever can be enough. When they reach their goals and still are cloaked in misery, some of them seek professional help.

What caused the mothers to emotionally mistreat their babies? Zahler explained: "Some seemed to have fairly intense postpartum depression. They were withdrawn and attended to their children with great difficulty. One mother had lost four children before her child was born, and she was in a constant panic in dealing with the child. Another was fairly sadistic with the child." The problem seemed not to be that the mothers were "otherwise preoccupied—no more than all mothers. But what is essential in terms of the clients I see is that the mother's withdrawal goes on long enough during a critical time so that the baby doesn't believe that she is going to come back. The object relationship and the constancy factors are very seriously disrupted, and the baby's emotional storage bank doesn't get filled up."

How many of these babies are only children driven to high achievement as adults is not known. But surely there are many.

Cheated Then, Angry Now

Yes, what happens in the early years is so critical, especially to only children, whose straight-line relationship with their parents is not obstructed by siblings. Psychiatrist Spurgeon English said that "the important thing is the way the children were treated when they were young—and during adolescence. If it was bad, they feel bad inside, and the bad feelings inevitably come out. 'I don't want to see you. I don't want to call you.' A lot of adult children call or visit their parents by obligation, not by choice or for pleasure. These children and their parents don't make each other feel good. When they meet, look each other in the eye, greet each other, they don't carry a good feeling. Very little goes on between them that is cheerful and rewarding."

Many parents feel that giving material things is being a good parent, that this can endear the child to them. But it doesn't work this way. "A lot of grown children are angry, or at least they feel resentful. They feel shortchanged, and they may not be conscious of the reasons why. They may find out when their own children are growing up, when they go to PTA meetings and hear discussions of what family life could be but wasn't for them. They begin to compare and they scream 'God, I really was shortchanged!' If we, as parents, don't meet their needs as children—play with them when they're little and be their friends when they're adolescents—they'll later give us the cool side, if not actively kick our behinds.

This is practically a law of life. This is what happens, and if you make up your mind to have a child, you better damn well have time for him, or you won't have a friend in your middle age and beyond."

— 10 —

Breaking the Chains of Dependency

To an extraordinary degree, the only child struggles to break away from home and become an independent person. Often the struggle is set up by parents who, despite honorable intentions, hold on too tightly and too long because they are painfully aware that the only child is "all we've got." Separating can be difficult on parents and children alike. Just ask Eleanor.

A sophomore at a college in the San Francisco Bay area, Eleanor feels that she finally has enough distance to keep her parents from getting more involved in her life than she wants them to be. Still, that distance didn't keep them away the first year. "They'd drive over from Sacramento just to spend a few hours, whether I invited them or not, and it got to be almost like it was when I was living at home, when they wanted to know everything I did and everything I thought. Finally, on one of the visits, I said to them 'Look, I feel a lot better about seeing you when we don't see each other so often.' My mother felt rejected and immediately went into the deep freeze, but I think my father really understood. The visits are much less frequent now, and things were different when I was home last summer. They gave me more space."

Eleanor said that she felt overprotected as she was growing up. "They took a lot of my responsibility and made a lot of decisions for me, and that stunted my independence in some ways. But I'm not bitter about that. I understand, I think, how parents must feel about their only child. You become too precious to them. But they're acting out of love, and I love them for that. They've given me so much."

Was it difficult for Eleanor to confront her parents when she felt they were crowding her? Not as difficult as it might be for only children who had been brought up in a more authoritarian environment, she said. "My parents always encouraged me to say what was on my mind, and they never penalized me for it—even when what I said reflected negatively on them. Especially, my Dad, who'd say something like 'Well, honey, tell me more about how you feel about what we've been doing.' I have two girlfriends who are only children, and their parents wouldn't allow dissent at all. I remember being at Marti's house a couple of years ago, and she said something her mother didn't like, and her mother said 'If you're going to talk like that, I'd rather you kept quiet.' That's really devastating, and it's been more of a struggle for Marti than for me to get enough courage to ask for what she wants—especially for her parents to give her more space."

Still, it hasn't been easy for Eleanor. "My problem—that's a funny thing to call it—is that my parents have been so good to me, and they love me so much, and I love them. It's really hard for me to do anything that might hurt them or disappoint them."

Parents of only children do tend to be hurt and disappointed if they're asked to back off. But their children's emotional growth demands it.

A Different Kind of Struggle

Sometimes the only child finds it difficult to get out into the world and become independent not because of parents but because of ghosts. Peppy Ehrman knows all about ghosts.

She was named Pepa, in honor of her grandmother, when she was born in 1938 in the village of Leziansk, Poland, a ninety-minute drive from Warsaw. When World War II started the next year, her parents "moved to the eastern part of Poland that was given to the Russians," and, shortly after that, she and her parents were sent to Siberia as part of a labor force.

She can't remember any of that, of course, but they did talk about it later, she and her parents—about the isolation and desperation, the howling winds and the cold, the ice, the hopelessness. After eighteen months, they got out of Siberia by bribing some local officials and moved to a Russian village near the Afghanistan border, where they lived in a barracks "with lots of other people." Peppy can remember something about that, about playing with the many other children, about not having any privacy in the barracks . . .

When they moved back to Poland, "my parents worked all day, and I was like a street kid in a small village. I was frightened a lot of the time. I saw a lot of death around me, and I was terrified of losing my parents. That was my worst memory, of the terror. . . . There was a lot of talk at the dinner table, often just the three of us, and they talked to me like an adult. In some ways that was nice. I learned certain skills. But in other ways it was horrible. Some of it should have been censored, the things that were terrifying to a little girl. Some of the people who came to our house told us about the concentration camps, and I had nightmares about that. They'd talk so openly about who died and how, about starvation and deprivation. . . . Some of it was too much for me."

The family moved to Germany for two years and then in 1949, when Peppy was eleven, they came to live in the United States. "I was very dependent on my parents, very close to them. In many ways we were like good friends. My mother said that I was an only child by choice, that they couldn't imagine having another child under the circumstances back then, that it was enough to have one. But when we were in Germany, everybody was having children, and my parents didn't. So I'm not 100 percent sure. . . . After we got to this country, my parents worked hard. I saw less of them than in Germany, and I spent a lot of time alone, but I never was lonely. I was always a kid who had a lot of friends. I always had a best friend or two or three, wherever I was. I guess this was my substitute for not having siblings.

"When I was a kid, I never wanted siblings. I was conscious of it because people always asked, and I always said no. But after I got married and had a daughter, there was no question, by the time she was two or three, that I wanted more children, as much for her as for me. But at that point, it wasn't possible for me to have another child, and so here I was, an only child with an only child, even though I felt strongly that she should have brothers and sisters.

"The hard part for me was when she went away to college. I'd been divorced for four years then, and I felt so completely alone, like I had no function in my life. I'd go to school where I was teaching and see parents picking up their kids, and I'd cry. I'd come home, and that's when the real loneliness would hit me. The house was empty. I didn't cook. It didn't seem to matter if I came home or not. . . . I tried not to burden my daughter with this. I kept in touch with her. I telephoned. I told her it was hard for me, but I didn't describe the degree. I told her I missed her."

As her daughter was growing up, Peppy Ehrman "made a conscious decision that she was going to be more independent than I was. That was my shortcoming of being an only child. I was frightened to go very far from home, afraid of getting lost, literally. I had no sense of direction. I was aware of this fear and very unhappy with it, and I didn't want my daughter to be like that. When she was very young, we'd go into town, and I'd teach her how to do it alone the next time. She grew up as an independent person. When she was a junior in college, she went off to Europe by herself for several weeks. I never could have done that. The first time I did it was when I was forty, and I felt liberated. She did it at nineteen."

Peppy Ehrman said that it took many years of therapy for her to shed her dependency and to understand how it had come about, because of growing up as an only child in a world that temporarily had gone mad, where death was a daily companion, where in an instant parents could be taken away forever. But one legacy of her background is harder to eradicate: her fear of moving.

"We traveled so much when I was growing up, and the result is that I want to stay where I am forever. Having a house is very important to me. Not moving is more important. I hate moving. When I move, it brings up terrible feelings, and I become very anxious. I start connecting with the past. Any move is very difficult for me, even a pleasant move, a move I initiate and want. I'm still not free from my past. . . . I'm so envious of people who can pick up and move from one city to another. I wish I could do it, and someday I may have to."

She is married now to psychiatrist Paul Fink, and she accompanied him in 1987 to a world psychiatric conference in Poland, the first time she had been back to her native land since the war years. "We went back to my hometown. I have no memory of living there, but I know it's my home. Every little town has a square, and there are businesses around the square, and I stood there, knowing that I was born in one of those houses above one of those stores that belonged to my father. . . . One of those houses was mine. I was trying to connect to something that was a home, but I couldn't."

A Lesson Learned Well

Psychologist Carol Gantman maintains that independence is a two-sided issue for only children. "Most people think of only children as being independent, and they are—as far as their relationships with peers. But only children are very dependent on adults. They come into a room filled with adults and children, and only children are more likely to gravitate toward the adults. They're more comfortable around adults, and they need adult attention, which, I suspect, is why they're achievement-oriented. They're trying to please their parents, and later on their teachers, their bosses, their Army sergeants. The only child's great respect for authority reflects the powerful influence of the parents. The child learns, quite early, that these other authority figures are extensions of the parents. The mother takes the child to school, and it's as if the gavel has been passed to the teacher. 'Now do what the teacher says.' It's the transfer of authority from one adult to another," and it's a lesson that the only child learns well.

Because of their dependence on adults and their need to please, only children carry an enormous sense of responsibility and loyalty that at times can hinder their breaking away and leading their own lives without guilt or regret.

Layton H. Fireng, knows about the responsibility of the only child. He is technical director of Breakthrough Environments of Havertown, Pennsylvania, and is the designer of the firm's so-called quiet rooms that are used for relaxation by professional sports teams and by businesses that want employees to have a place to cool down and unwind. After his divorce in 1974, Fireng moved back into the family home and took care of his elderly mother. "I saw it as an obligation but not a burden. It's what you do as part of a family, and I never made a judgment about it. I never thought 'Someday this weight will be lifted.' I had some bones to pick with her . . . it wasn't a perfect relationship by any means, but she was my mother, a grand lady, and I loved her. . . . She was a very strong person, but near the end the roles got reversed, as they almost always do. I became the parent."

First and foremost, Fireng was his mother's keeper. After her death he made the necessary arrangements, and when he left the hospital to return to the family home, he recalled, "I couldn't get warm. I wrapped myself in blankets, but it was as if my bones were frozen."

That afternoon was sunny and warm, and Fireng went for a drive with a friend, with the sunroof open. "The sky had high rippling clouds, and there was an airplane flying high, but under the clouds. It looked special to me. I'd never seen an airplane like it. It was flying into the sunset, and I felt like a little boy. My mother was going away, in that airplane, and I didn't want her to go. It was a very strange experience. I can't explain what happened, but the roles were reversed once more. She was the mother again, and I was the little boy, sad, frightened, and dependent."

Psychologist William Liberi knows about responsibility . . . and loyalty, too.

When he was five years old, he developed a severe cold, and by midafternoon he was so sick that his mother took him to the doctor. After checking the little boy, the doctor reassured the mother: "He'll be all right. It'll take some time for him to be back to normal, but you don't have to worry." They went home, but the illness, in a flash, became worse. Liberi's skin started to turn blue, and his mother frantically called another doctor, who came to their house and after a quick examination announced: "It's bronchial pneumonia, and we've got to get to the hospital fast!" He had perhaps an hour to live, unless . . .

They piled into the doctor's car—there was no time to call an ambulance—and they sped to the emergency room, where doctors performed a tracheotomy. He would recover, as good as new, but it had been a close call and his mother was frazzled from the strain. The little boy held her hand and sought to reassure her: "Don't worry, Mom. If I die, I'll come back to take care of you."

Years later Liberi would recall that story and explain what it meant: "It was an ethnic family, Italian, very much relationship-oriented, where people mattered, where nothing was more important than good relationships. Loyalty was very important, too, and I got some very strong messages about it. What I was saying to my mother, as an only child of five, was that I knew about loyalty and responsibility and that I was going to do what was expected of me."

Looking for an Escape Hatch

The only child who has profound difficulty breaking away and becoming his own person is the child of the boss in a family-owned business. For this child it's often next to impossible to escape being trapped in the business as an adult, even if he or she doesn't like it. Peter Davis and Edward Kuljian, who directed workshops on family-held businesses at the University of Pennsylvania's Wharton School, told me that it's not uncommon for the child never to look into other career possibilities because of parental expectations and the built-in security represented by the business. With this lack of preparation for anything else, the child is not able at twenty-five or forty-five, if disenchantment strikes, to go out and do something else.

Even if the child wants to do something else, he may be challenged by the entrepreneurial makeup of the father, said Kuljian. "The entrepreneur personality is great at making you feel guilty. 'Why do you think I sacrificed all these years? It's your business now—so don't tell me that you don't want it!' The entrepreneur doesn't like people to desert him. He tends to look upon them as absolute traitors, and he can make life miserable for them." That's the bad news. Now here's even worse news.

"For the entrepreneur, it may be difficult to handle the son's success. The entrepreneur may be ambivalent about it. On the one hand, he wants the son to succeed because the son one day is going to handle the business. But on the other hand, the son's success can be a nail in the old man's coffin, and he doesn't like that. The result of this can be a mixed message from father to son: Succeed, but not too much."

Alice is twenty-three, an only child, and her *handicap*—that's her word for it—is that she is a woman. "I spend time wondering if I'll ever be the person my father is now—my father, who runs the company and who is my boss. I know that one day I will be faced with the responsibility of running the family business as successfully as my father has done in the past. The problem is that a daughter has to work twice as hard as a son to prove that she is worthy of filling her father's shoes. We must convince others that our sex is not a handicap and, while we're doing this, we also must prove our capabilities. It's a big job, uphill all the way."

I asked Kuljian just how tough it is for a female only child to follow her father into the family business. "There's no question that more and more women are entering family businesses. In our seminars, out of a group of fifteen or sixteen we'll get four or five women, almost twenty-five or thirty percent. . . . Women do have special problems, but in some ways the problems are advantages, too. I don't say this in a deprecating way, but a daughter often tends to be daddy's 'little girl,' and he may not breathe down her neck as hard as he would with a son. My wife and I have one child, a daughter, and as I see her grow up, it occurs to me how frequently fathers are demanding and tough on the son to toe the line, meet the standard. They don't indulge the son, and they make him go out and get jobs in his early teens to find out what the world is like. But I think you frequently find that fathers are very indulgent with their daughters, and sometimes the relationship is less competitive."

In other words, fathers may tend to demand less perfection from the daughter who follows them into the business than from the son. "I think the father makes definite concessions for the daughter and in a business context a father's seeing a daughter as heiress apparent in the family business can be a real advantage. While a lot of fathers can remain competitive with the son and feel challenged by the son, the father with a daughter often has a certain pride in what the daughter is doing in the business, almost a boastfulness: 'Gosh, look at how my daughter is running things.' "

But nobody seriously doubts that the only child in the family business, male or female, has a difficult time establishing independence, an identity apart from the family. Kuljian said that he has known adult children who wrecked the family business in order to escape—because they knew of no other way to get out on their own. That's an expensive way to do it, and it's a very dramatic illustration of the depth of the passion to "be my own person, do my own thing."

Parents Who Cling . . . and Cling

Sarah thought it would be therapeutic to write me a letter about a subject that, over the years, I had written so much about: the difficulty that many parents have in turning loose their adult only children. "There are parents, with their unbending attitudes, who forever stress the obligation owed to them by the child. My mother, who passed away a few months ago, was one of them. I am forty-six years old, and it has taken me much of my life to come out from under this kind of philosophy. I have come to feel that what the child owes the parents is: respect, if they have earned it; love, if they have given it; communication, if they are willing to listen as well as speak. These parents will tell you that they love their child, but what they really do is want to control everything their child does. Whenever I complain to friends about the behavior and attitude of our parents, some of them counter with the argument that we, too, will be like that when we are older. But I know that we will not be the same, because my husband and I already have raised our child differently. We have not used fear or intimidation. . . . If our child has a good, fulfilling life, we will be happy and feel that we have succeeded as parents. And we won't need to lean on our child to visit us, write us and telephone us to make us feel good about ourselves. . . . If from my hard experience as an only child I could pass along one piece of advice, it would be this: Live your life independently without giving in to guilt feelings caused by your parents' constant pleas for attention.

With many parents, the child could be with them twenty-four hours a day, three hundred sixty-five days a year, and this still wouldn't be enough."

Sarah's letter made me think back to one of the final conversations I had with my mother. "I get so many letters from adult only children about parents who almost suffocate them with requests for attention. It makes me realize all over again how fortunate I am to have had you and Dad as parents, because from both of you I never felt anything but acceptance and encouragement. I'm not going to belabor the point, but I do want you to know how much I appreciate everything that you both did for me."

Mom let all of it soak in, then she thanked me. "But, honestly, I don't know why you make such a big deal out of it. Dad and I weren't exceptional parents. All we ever did was love you."

The two women looked as if they could be sisters, dark-haired, in their middle twenties. They sat on the side of the steaming whirlpool in the health club and talked to each other about what seemed to be their common problem: a mother's reluctance to loosen her grasp, to treat her children not as babies but as adults.

"She still tells me when to wear my raincoat, not to go outside with my hair wet, to be sure to eat right, to get plenty of rest. I know she's concerned, but I wish to God she'd find another way to show it. She can't leave me alone. I hope I'm never like that, if I have a child."

The other woman ventured that it was a mother's way "of being a mother. She doesn't know any other way to act."

"How does a mother get like that?"

"By being a mother, instead of a woman."

It's true, said psychologist Matti Gershenfeld, that the parents who have the most trouble turning loose their adult child are those who have sizable ego needs that tend to be met primarily through that child. "For some parents, the greatest achievement of their lives is their child. The highlight of their week is when the child comes to their house for Sunday dinner."

Tragically, some parents seem to strive to create and maintain their child's dependency on them. "When the child was small, parents used reward and punishment to get him to behave as they wanted him to. If he ate all of his spinach, he got ice cream for dessert. Now that the child is grown, this is continued, but in a different way. The parents try to bribe their child through buying him a car, a washing machine, a sofa. It's a manipulative strategy that seeks to keep the parents in control with promises. Then, if the child doesn't do what the parents want, he doesn't get the car or the sofa or whatever. This either creates dependence or hatred, but usually it's hatred."

How Much Does the Adult Only Child Owe the Parents?

It was obvious from the handwriting—and from the tone of the letter—that the woman was elderly:

> I'm writing to tell you that I'd like to talk to you. I would like to talk to you about what responsibility children have to their parents—children who are thirty-five or forty years old and whose parents are between seventy and eighty. Mostly, it seems to me, the son with his doctoral degree has forgotten the sacrifices his parents made to give him the opportunity to be a success. Would you be kind enough to come to my house one of these days so that I could talk personally with you about this?

She was seventy-seven, and she had grown up as one of eight children in a European family in which closeness "never really was possible" because sheer numbers worked against it. In her mind she created a fantasy of an ideal family relationship—one in which people "would not just be nice but be genuine and loving." It was a fantasy that she brought with her when she and her husband came to America so many years ago. They had a son, who now was thirty-eight, and the mother's words were at first tender and then bitter as she described him. "He was my prince. From the very first day he taught me to love. To my son Mom was beautiful." The fantasy had become reality . . . but not for long. "At eleven he began to criticize me, and at sixteen he began to get away from us. My husband and I thought it was normal, and maybe it is. Unfortunately, maybe it is."

The son became a man, received his doctoral degree and became a faculty member at a big university in the Midwest. The mother, by now a widow, discovered she had cancer three years ago and underwent surgery, which seemed to be successful. At the time she was terrified—as anybody would be—and she cried out to her son for help. "I called him and said 'Joe, I need you,' but the line was silent. I said 'Joe, I want you to come here for a few days and be with me.' But he said nothing. The next day I called again, and I got the same no answer. I said 'Joe, one day you'll feel guilty about this.' That's when it hit me—about my fantasy of the perfect family relationship. If I dropped dead, nobody would know it. . . . He would call me, but there was a certain detachment. He was not with me. He was nice like a nephew but not loving like a son. This always was between us, this detachment. I went to therapy because I was crying all night, and I'm not the crying type. They told me that I should forget about my son, that our children are ours only until they don't need us any more. I blew up at that, but I'm afraid the therapists were right. . . . When my son calls, he tells me to 'go to your friends.' But my friends are old, too. When they play bridge, they want to have fun, not hear about somebody's problems. My son doesn't have to love me, but there should be compassion. I can't demand love, but I should be able to demand compassion."

It was a sad story—no doubt about that—and I pursued it. How often did she see her son? Well, he and his wife come to visit two or three times a year. She visits them in the Midwest, too, at least once a year, and the son pays for her airfare. There are telephone calls, too, but . . .

I was beginning to feel that maybe the story wasn't so sad after all. I asked the woman if the visits and telephone calls didn't suggest to her that the son had some loving feelings toward her. Yes, maybe, but she needed more. She wanted open expressions of love because "older people need the security of feeling that they belong, that they are loved." She didn't get that from her son, she said.

Had she ever told her son that she was not satisfied with their relationship? No, but "he knows it." How could she be sure? "Because a mother knows these things." I told her that if I wrote anything about our conversation, I could expect to get letters from angry parents who would like to trade places with her, angry parents who seldom even got letters from their grown children, let alone several visits each year. Had she ever considered that she was better off in the relationship with her son than she thought? Had she ever considered the possibility that her expectations were not realistic, that a grown son couldn't reasonably be expected to keep his mother on center stage all of his life?

Yes, she knew that many other mothers might be thrilled to get a birthday card from a son, but that wasn't enough for her. "Once, when he was little, I had the whole cake. Now I have only crumbs, and I'm not satisfied with crumbs." As a mother, she had "given, given, and given to him, but now I'm supposed to be satisfied with what I get back." It wasn't fair, she complained.

I found myself siding with the son—even though he had not responded to his mother's cry for help when she was ill. Perhaps I identified with him because his mother was only a year older than my mother was when she died, my mother who lived 1,500 miles away and who so often told me that the two letters I wrote every week and my annual visit were not crumbs but essential parts of her life. The most important thing I could do for her, she had said, was to carve out a happy, satisfying life for myself, and to share with her and to love her. When I told the woman about that, she didn't seem impressed. Her son "used to say so easily 'I love you' to me. But now he can't seem to say that any more."

I suggested that she give him time. At thirty-eight I had great difficulty telling my parents that I loved them, but later I had no difficulty at all. It was a joy—because it meant so much to them, and I felt it so deeply. The woman wasn't sure that she had much time to wait. What she was sure of was that life hadn't treated her fairly. I thought of a story that my mother used to tell about elderly people who complain but who don't do anything to try to fix what's wrong. I started to share the story, but I didn't—because I didn't believe that the woman would want to hear it or would be able to understand it.

When I left her home, I wasn't sure that it had been wise for me to visit. I'm pretty sure that she felt the same way.

Many years ago a psychiatrist told me something that I think should be used by parents as a reality check when they get confused about how their children respond to them. What the psychiatrist said was this: Children always mean more to parents than parents mean to children. I believe that this is true, and I believe it from my perspective both as an adult child and as the father of two adult sons. As much as I loved my mother and father, I don't think that it approached their love for me. They saved every letter that I wrote to them—but they didn't make a big deal out of that. They didn't make a deal out of it at all. I found the letters, hundreds of them, as I was emptying the house after Mom's death. Some of them dated back to 1962, when I left home to go to Louisville. That was symbolic to me of how much I meant to them.

From the other end of the relationship, as a father, I find myself at the beginning of each new year writing down my sons' birth-dates in my calendar—so that I can't possibly forget, since I'm so bad at remembering dates—and even scrawling reminders of when it's time to get their gifts or checks in the mail. Many times I don't hear from them on my birthday. I don't think this means they don't love me, but it does indicate they lack the urgency I feel to let them know how special they are to me on their special days. I'm sure they mean more to me than I mean to them, and that's the way it is, a natural happening. It's something parents should keep in mind if they feel the need to call their adult only child to task for not remembering something that is important to them. And it's something the adult only child needs to understand if the parents do complain.

What do adult only children owe their parents? What is reasonable for parents to expect?

These are complicated questions today, said psychologist Edward B. Fish, but in yesteryears things were plain and simple. "A boy was expected to follow in his father's footsteps. A girl was expected to marry and have children, and in that respect she followed in her mother's footsteps. To a great extent, roles were designated and rules were laid down. The parents got old and expected the child to care for them, perhaps even take them into his home . . . because the child always paid back the parents."

One of the reasons things are so complicated today is due to what Fish described as "the pressure of upward mobility." Parents often push and shove their child to be all that he can be—and then some—and the result not infrequently is tremendous resentment by the child. In so many families the child "is expected to move ahead and surpass the parents in education, career, income. Parents expect the child to continue at an accelerated pace that the parents themselves had when they surpassed their parents. But there's a limit to what is realistic to expect, and the child, when he's pushed so much, tends to rebel." One of the ways in which the child rebels is by doing the opposite of what the parents want in everything from education to career choices to marriage.

In the process of rebellion, a breach is created in the relationship, and often it's difficult to patch, especially in a mobile society in which the only child may live a thousand miles from the parents. As a generalization, said Fish, "If the child has a good relationship with parents, the child will go through life doing the kinds of things that please parents . . . because these things become part of the child's values. If the relationship is bad, the child will go through life fighting parents, doing things to aggravate them."

Fish said it's reasonable for an adult only child to treat parents "the way a good friend is treated. It's reasonable to maintain contact, to let parents know that they can depend on you in a crunch, to assure them that you'll visit if they are ill. It's reasonable to love them and give to them, but at the same time to look out for yourself."

Fish had a few words for parents of an adult only child: It's *not* reasonable to expect to continue the parent-child relationship as it once was, when the child regarded them as all-wise and all-powerful. That's not a healthy relationship for anybody when the child is grown, and parents who try to cling to it are riding a fast track to alienation from their child. It's important for parents to understand that there is no way that they ever can be repaid for the love, time, effort, money and worry they poured into bringing up their child. "You can't ever get your money back. Dollar for dollar, it's not a fair exchange. If you expect a fair exchange, you'll likely be disappointed. But if you gave from love, you'll likely get more rewards later than if you were conscious of what you were giving and expected a fifty-percent yield on your investment."

What happens when the only child marries and moves away? What then is appropriate behavior for the child? It's appropriate for the child to remain concerned about the parents, said Fish, "in a healthy way. At this point, parents have moved from the center to the periphery of the child's life, but the child shouldn't disown parents. . . . Parents have a right to be remembered on occasions, to be included in a peripheral kind of way." The child should give parents "the feeling that they're still important and not do things to make them feel they've outlived their purpose."

But all of this, said Fish, assumes maturity in the parents and the child, and this can be a doubtful assumption. "Probably we're talking about a small percentage of people. We assume that mature parents will have a mature child and mature relationships, but a lot of parents don't want their child to grow up and succeed. They want the child always to be dependent and subservient. A lot of fathers want to be able to say to a son at forty: 'You'll never be the man I was.' If parents are neurotic in what they want, their neurotic needs will follow them to the grave, and their child never will be able to do enough for them."

But What If . . .

My parents didn't cling to me and didn't encourage me to be dependent on them or to look to them as my only source of nourishment. Yet, I had a terrible time breaking away from home. Why? Mostly it was because I enjoyed a good life there—not in a material way, although I got whatever goodies were available, but from the standpoint of being accepted, listened to, treated with respect, made to feel important.

When I ventured into the outside world, to go away to college thirty miles away on a football scholarship, I was frightened and often homesick. I went through rush week, and I was asked to pledge by two fraternities, but I turned down both of them. Why? I wouldn't be able to go home on weekends because pledges had weekend chores to do. Nothing was going to keep me from going home, and my parents, while they didn't especially encourage it, always seemed happy to see me—and that was encouragement enough. When they took me back to the football dormitory on Sunday nights, I always felt sad. I'd kiss them goodbye, shoulder my bag of clean laundry, walk down the quiet hallway to my dark room . . . and cry softly and remind myself that in just five days I'd be able to go home again. I never told anybody about that, not even my parents, because on some level I suppose I was ashamed of it. How could a highly recruited football player cry about something like that?

When I was drafted into the Army, I was stationed seventy-five miles from home at Fort Leonard Wood, Missouri. After basic training, I went home every weekend and, when I bought my first car, I sometimes even went home during the week, for some home cooking . . . and some nurturing . . . and to visit friends with whom I had grown up.

Two things made possible a change in my outlook. The first was that as I became more comfortable with myself and more successful in my career, I got more and more goodies from other people in other places. The second was that I took a job, at Dad's urging, four hundred miles away, and while I missed being home at first, even though I was married, I began to enjoy the independence.

In the beginning what I learned was about as far removed from true independence as it's possible to get. I felt that to be independent I had to ignore my parents, not write too often, not call them without a specific reason, not visit more than once a year and, when I did visit, to spend as much time as possible on the golf course. This kind of behavior hurt my parents deeply, and it wasn't until years later that I was truly mature enough and independent enough to talk with them about why I had acted that way.

True independence, I learned, is not ignoring your parents. True independence is loving them enough to do some of what it takes to make them happy, without sacrificing your own integrity or needs. True independence is being able to exercise freedom of choice. Understanding this was a profound breakthrough for me, and when I shared it with Mom and Dad, they seemed so pleased—far more pleased, as I recall, than they ever seemed when I went home to visit every weekend.

—— 11 ——

Parenting the Only Child

Aaron is forty-nine years old, an accountant, neatly buttoned down in his gray flannel suit—to all the world a man who knows who he is and where he's going. Yet, although he conceals it well, Aaron often feels like a little boy who presses his nose against the window and wishes that he would be invited to go outside and play with the other kids.

Aaron is like a lot of only children who, raised by adoring parents, got first-rate instruction in what the parents thought was important and when he went to kindergarten was miles ahead of everybody else in these "important" things. He could count to infinity; he could write numbers; he could recite the alphabet; he could spell words; he could compose sentences. But what Aaron didn't know how to do was act his age. He couldn't communicate with the other kids because he talked not like a five-year-old but like an adult, and they made fun of him. He didn't know how to put blocks together; he couldn't catch or throw a ball; he'd never heard of the games that kids routinely played. Most of all, he couldn't get along with the other kids. He didn't know how to share things, how to tell funny stories, how to fall down and laugh at himself, how to cooperate, how to stand up for himself, how to fight and make up.

Aaron had learned adult skills from his parents, but he had not learned childhood skills. If there is one overriding message that needs to be understood by parents of only children, it is this: Don't ever forget that they are children, and resist the temptation, even though you spend so much time together, to turn them into little adults. They'll grow up fast enough, so parents owe it to their children and to themselves to take steps to make the childhood experience as rich as possible.

What should parents do? As much as they can, they should expose their only child to other children who are about the same age. They should invite other children from the neighborhood in to play and, in the words of psychiatrist Pirooz Sholevar, "treat everybody as equals, as part of the family. What you're trying to do is create a family situation" by using somebody else's children. Leon Katz, an only child, said that his mother seemed to feel a responsibility "to hook me up with other kids, to see that I had somebody to play with. If there was another only child in the neighborhood, she'd visit the mother and suggest that the children become friends." Parents should make it a point to bring in babysitters, to maintain areas of their lives that don't include their only child. This is one important way in which parents can help the only child to understand that life exists outside his own little universe. At the same time they are helping the child to become more independent.

Aaron is not bitter about what happened to him. Rather, he is philosophical. "They helped me with my homework, because that's what they understood. But they never invited a friend along when we went on vacation so I'd have company my own age. They didn't understand that. 'You'll be with us, Aaron, the three of us, and we'll have a good time.' That was the message, and, God knows, they meant well, but as a practical matter I never had much exposure to other kids and, in school, I didn't know how to act. So I studied and achieved . . . and I was thoroughly miserable . . .

"I remember once when my father, for whatever reason, learned a couple of judo throws, and he showed them to me. It was really out of character for him, and it was the only time anything like that ever happened, but it was so great . . . I felt like Superman! There was this kid around the corner, six years older, who was a real bully and who ridiculed me and called me a sissy. Even though I was frightened, I decided that I was going to stand up to him. The next time I saw him, he pushed me against a wall and started to pound on me, but I used one of the judo tricks. I took his arm, spun him around and tripped him. He went down, flat on his back, and I'll always remember the look on his face, absolute amazement. There was another kid there, and he started laughing, and the bully got up and chased him, but he never bothered me again after that.

"I always thought that if my father had spent more time with me at that level, teaching me things that boys needed to know, my life would have been different. . . . If I had learned to handle myself better then, I'd be more secure now, and I wouldn't have to struggle so hard to appear to be like everybody else. You know what I wish? I wish I could walk into a room filled with people and blend in comfortably, but I can't—even today. I have to act the role, and I can do that, but it's hard work."

Selma Kramer, a child psychiatrist, understood completely what Aaron was saying. She said that parents "can make the child into a little adult, but they can't teach him how to be a child. . . . I once had in treatment an only child who, at age five, could go into a restaurant and order from a French menu. He dressed like a member of royalty. . . . But he didn't know what to do if another kid bopped him, shoved him, crowded into line ahead of him." He was a classic little adult, and the only child is at some considerable risk of this, especially if the parents are older.

Related to the "little adult" is the child that Kramer calls the "messiah," who typically arrives after a long period of parental infertility, who clearly is the one and only child, who gets too much adoration, not enough frustration, and who, sadly, is made to bypass most of the things that children are supposed to do. "This one child is *it*. The parents know it and they're so overly protective. Physical activity often is restricted because it is seen as too dangerous," and the child is set apart from his peers. In fact, the "messiah" has no peers.

"This boy came into therapy with me at fifteen. He didn't know how to ride a bicycle or roller-skate or anything. His parents were afraid he might get hurt, and they passed their fears along to him. He was out of sync with children his age. It was terrible. He never felt like one of the guys. He was late into high school before he started to hang out with anybody his age. He didn't know the language, the raunchy words that he'd never heard at home. He didn't know when the guys called him the equivalent of a nerd if he should get mad or laugh."

At seventeen, after two years of therapy, the young man learned to ride a bicycle and to rollerskate, and he began to interact with those his own age. His parents, with Kramer's stout urging, went away on a week's vacation and left him behind, for the first time ever. It was progress, long overdue, but progress nonetheless.

The first cousin of the "messiah" is the "replacement" child, and, said Kramer, it is to this child that the cruelest legacy of all is passed. This is the child who is conceived as a replacement for a child who died and who, regardless of what he does, never is recognized by the parents as quite the equal of the lost child who is overidealized, almost deified. Parents burden the replacement child with many of their needs. They ask him to be everything to them, but in all ways they constantly remind him that he is number two.

"Replacement kids have a deep sense of inferiority, no matter how good they are. They can't match up with the dead child, although they try. They hate the role. They really hate it. . . . Physicians often say to parents after their child's funeral: 'Go home and make another baby.' I've seen children born nine months after the funeral. The parents mourn all through the pregnancy, and if they ever acknowledged that they were getting any pleasure, it might upset their vision of themselves as mourning parents. It's an awful load for a child to carry, not to bring any happiness to the parents. . . . The parents are overconcerned about the child's health and safety, especially if the first child died of illness or in an accident," and the replacement child, like the "messiah," is out of step with other children from the very beginning. Not much is written about this, said Kramer, and parents and even physicians tend to be unaware of the consequences for the child. The consequences, she stressed, can be severe . . . and never-ending.

The Importance of Recognizing Importance

All parents are important to their children, but to the only child parents are especially important. Their influence, to a large extent, is undiluted because there are no siblings around to water it down. This is an enormous responsibility, and a lot of parents want to duck it.

Michael DeSisto is a longtime educator who is executive director of the DeSisto Schools in Massachusetts and Florida. In his view, many parents share a common problem: They refuse to let themselves believe that they are the most important people in the lives of their children. The result: They often come up short in giving their children what the children most need—validation and acceptance.

"We're brought up not to think of ourselves as being this important. It's scary to believe, and it seems egotistical. . . . I was doing a seven-day workshop for parents, some of them powerful, successful businesspeople. When they began to realize how much their children adored them, when they began to take in what that meant, they were terrified. This level of responsibility—being so important to their children—makes parents uncomfortable," even parents who routinely take on crushing career responsibilities without flinching.

"You take the kid who's an overachiever. It's necessary for parents to recognize that most of what the child does is to please them, to live up to their standards. So this overachiever is striving for approval, but he doesn't get it and in frustration he begins to act out. Why doesn't he get it? Because the parents don't realize how important their approval is. When parents don't realize their kid needs it, the message they send to the kid is 'Hey, nothing you do is good enough.' Parents have got to be excited about what their child does. It's important for parents to say 'That's enough; you're okay; I am pleased.' If the child is struggling, it's important for parents to recognize it. 'Golly, I bet you feel awful. What can I do to help?' We've got to realize how central we are to our children."

The High Cost of Disappointment

Psychologist Sidney J. Cohen was talking about parents who try to make their children perfect—a situation that can be exaggerated with an only child, on whose shoulders all parental expectation falls.

"There are two different ways in which parents approach this. One way is blatant. The parents tell the child over and over that he must get all A's in school, must do exactly what is expected of him at home, must prepare himself to go to the right college to become a doctor or lawyer or whatever. . . . It's stated in a way in which there's no room left for discussion or negotiation. It's stated virtually as a matter of fact, and it's not stated warmly. It's stated repeatedly, from an early age. . . . If the child, at some age, says that he doesn't want to be a doctor or lawyer, the parent may respond 'This is what I want, and this is how it's going to be.' Or, more likely, the parent will respond with sarcasm. 'So you think you're going to do what *you* want, eh? Well, we'll see about that.' And the kid is left with the idea that he really has no choice. It's his life, but he has no choice."

The other way in which parents demand perfection is more insidious because it's subtle, with mixed messages to the child from one or both parents. "The parents say 'Gee, it doesn't matter at all if you don't succeed at this, just as long as you try your best.' But then they become very critical or disappointed if the child in fact does whatever it is imperfectly. . . . The kid comes home with less than all A's and the parents say 'Oh, that's OK,' but the tone of voice or facial expression makes it clear that it's not OK." In both cases—blatant or subtle—the result tends to be the same: a confused, often rebellious child and disappointed, often angry parents.

Why would parents do this to the child they love, demand the child be perfect? Not infrequently, said Cohen, it's a pathetic attempt to get their children to make up for their own shortcomings. It's a fact that many parents are disappointed in themselves and consciously or unconsciously want their children to erase that disappointment. When this burden is not spread out over several children and falls on an only child, the result can be devastating.

"There are many possible areas in which people can feel disappointed, and it could be any or all of them—academically, professionally, socially, physically, in relationships with the family. . . . Any parent who is disappointed in any or all of these areas is likely, whether aware of it or not, to try to make the child perfect in those areas. . . . If one parent is also disappointed with the other parent in some of these areas, there's even more onus on the child to fill the void, to be perfect. . . . If you're disappointed with yourself and your spouse, too, it's literally a double whammy" for the child who, no matter what happens, probably won't be able to satisfy the parents' expectations.

The child tends to react at one of two extremes. "One extreme is that the child constantly strives for perfection. If he gets an A minus, he feels very disappointed. In his activities—sports, music or whatever—the slightest mistake causes him to come home and hang his head for hours. The slightest disappointment is blown up into a major failure." The other extreme is acting out his resentment of the parental attitude by opposition and/or rebellion. The child tries to do exactly the opposite of what the parents want.

For the most part, said Cohen, parents are aware of what they're doing—even though they often are unaware of why they're doing it, which is to compensate for their own feelings of inadequacy. Often, if they're asked why, they will say something like this: "Well, if our child does what we tell him to do, he'll grow up to be a great person. We're doing it for his own good." A challenge for these parents is to get in touch with their real motivation, and here is how Cohen suggests they do it: "Ask yourself how satisfied or dissatisfied you honestly are in each of those areas—academically, professionally, socially, physically, in family relationships. If you're disappointed, if you feel that you should have done better in any of those areas, this virtually guarantees that you'll convey it to your child."

Cohen counsels many parents who are trying to force their children to make up for what they themselves didn't achieve. "This guy will come in and tell me 'Sid, I'm disappointed in my profession' or in his marriage or with his friends, and he'll say something like 'The worst part is that I don't know what the hell to do about it.' And so then I get more information on how he's dealing with his child, and almost inevitably, he's putting a lot of pressure on the child to make up for his shortcomings. If the parent says 'My kid's got a problem,' usually he's implicitly or explicitly saying 'But I, as a parent, am not the problem.' So I get more information on how the kid is a problem, and almost always this leads into areas where the kid is not performing up to expectations," which tend to be skewed by the parents' own real or perceived failures.

Are there times when it's appropriate for parents to express their disappointment to their child? Yes, said Cohen, it's appropriate after parents have fulfilled these three responsibilities: They have set good examples for identifying and resolving problems and being successful in the projects that they undertake; they have been good role models for honesty, "especially about feelings," if they mean what they say and say what they mean; they have "consistently done the first two things but the child still repeatedly succumbs to detrimental peer influence."

Parents who have done these things are in a position to convey their disappointment directly, without beating around the bush or sounding apologetic. "Parents have to say more than 'I am disappointed.' To leave it at that is not enough. It would make the kid feel guilty, and that's not constructive. A parent could say 'I am disappointed, and the reason is that I feel, as your parent, that I practice what I preach. I do as I say. I'm telling you that the key to getting where you want is to work hard and to persist. The key to getting close to people is to be honest. I'm telling you and modeling it, but you continue not to do it. You give in to friends, and I think you're smart enough to know it's hurting you.' It's totally appropriate to convey this to any kid who's old enough to understand your words."

What kind of reaction might be expected from the child? "If he's a teenager, the reaction could be on-the-spot defensiveness or silence. Either of these extremes would reflect that the kid did not want to admit at the moment that what you were saying was true. For the kid to say 'Gee, Dad, you're right,' would be earth-shaking . . . but defensiveness or silence doesn't mean that what you're saying has fallen on deaf ears or has been disregarded. It may mean that the kid will take a few days to let it all sink in."

How often is it appropriate to repeat the message, if nothing seems to change in the child's behavior? "If you make clear what you expect and continue to role-model it and if the kid continues not to carry through, then reminders are appropriate every couple of months. . . . If the kid is still school-age, as opposed to being grown up, it's reasonable to talk about certain punishments for not working hard, for not getting the grades he's capable of getting."

I asked Cohen if there is a "best" way for parents to try to get the child to do what they want the child to do—without conveying the message that the child is being coerced and left without choice. Especially, I wondered about careers, since so many only children have complained to me that their parents virtually made the decision for them.

"The message that has to be given is 'Look, I need to be honest with you. It is important to me. It would mean a lot to me if you would continue this tradition. But at the same time I have to face the fact that when you're an adult, you have the right to make your own choice. I will try to respect your choice if it's not to keep up the tradition. But I'll be honest: I hope you keep it up.' I would suggest doing it this way as opposed to saying that the child really has no choice."

Cohen said "The irony is that a lot of times if you present the kid with a choice but if you let him know what you prefer, you likely will undercut any rebellion and increase the chance that the kid will do what you want."

I asked Cohen what is an appropriate way for a child or young adult to respond to parents who seem to be trying to force their will on him. "I think that the kid has to sit the parents down, muster up all the courage he can find, look them in the eye and say something like 'Please, Mom and Dad, I need you to understand that I need to make my own choice and that if I choose something different, it's nothing personal against you.' Parents may not buy it, but they need to hear it. The kid may have to repeat it a few times" before parents understand that it's for real and that the child isn't going to back off.

Then There Is the Princess

It's called the "princess syndrome," and it can produce a woman who, in the words of psychiatrist Leo Madow, is "hell on wheels. She's hell in a relationship, demanding, difficult if not impossible to please. A pretty girl, especially if she is the only child, is in danger of becoming a princess," and it is quite a danger.

Psychologist Carol Gantman said parents who bring up a daughter as a princess don't realize that they are creating a monster—in the sense that the child, even when she's grown, tends to know only one thing: how to receive. "The girl was not raised with that intent . . . but a day of reckoning comes on down the line. . . . I see a lot of women who are struggling to be independent emotionally and financially. There's a strong pull from the parents for them to come back home—'We'll take care of you.' So the woman's plumbing leaks and she calls Daddy, who sends over his plumber. This is the disadvantage of a protected childhood. You don't learn you can take care of things yourself. Parents want to anticipate needs before needs arrive, and the child doesn't know how to solve problems. The parents have good intentions," but the net result is that they tend to produce spoiled, helpless daughters who, when they get married, merely transfer dependency from their fathers to their husbands and expect to have things taken care of, often without their even asking.

What kind of man marries a princess? It would be rare for him to be an only child because, as an only child, he is very likely to be more comfortable as the sole center of attention, a prince in his own right, accustomed like the princess not to giving but to receiving. No, the man who marries a princess is seeking something else. Said Gantman: "A princess looks good; she provides a good image in the way she creates the family and the home. It's easier for a man to be part of it superficially. The kids always are well dressed and well mannered, and home is a nice place to bring the boss. In that sense she offers a lot. She's safe and not threatening. She receives material goods, and in return she creates a good environment and creature comforts for the husband. This appeals to a man who doesn't want a heavy-duty relationship."

Turning Loose, with Love . . . and with Pain

The mother stared through the one-way glass and watched her three-year-old son play with the other children. No question about it: He was busy, and he seemed happy. He wrestled somebody for possession of a plastic firefighter's hat. Then he tugged on a yellow balloon that floated on a string. He marched to the table for a slice of "pizza" that he and his playmates had helped make. He drank his apple juice, then asked for more.

She watched, this mother of her first and probably only child. She is on the shy side of middle age, a professional woman who put her career on a back burner because she wanted to be with her child full-time and "get him off to the best start he could have." She was happy that her son was doing so well, that he played so easily with the other children. "He's very secure. He loves being with the other children." But she also acknowledged mixed feelings. "It's sad to see him do so well without me. It's almost like he's doing *too* well . . . I want him to be independent, but I feel really sad. I'm losing somebody. For three years he was solely dependent on me. Now I'm giving up control, and it's the beginning of our growing apart. That feels sad. It's a big loss to start sharing him with other people."

The woman was among a dozen mothers who had enrolled themselves and their children in a popular program called So Long, Mom at Pennsylvania Hospital in Philadelphia—a program designed to smooth the separation of mother and child, a separation that invariably appears to be more difficult for the mother than for the child. What makes it so difficult? The answer, said the program's director, Gail Loeb, is that the mother feels cut out as the primary influence in the child's life. "It's the loss of the parental role, and it's hard to turn loose, especially if it's a role that the parent likes."

Parenting has been described as the only job in which the object is to put yourself out of business—by preparing your child to leave home, when the time is right, and live independently.

If this is the heartbeat of good parenting, and I think it is, then it must be said that many parents are coming up short by encouraging their child to remain dependent on them, whether or not they realize it, long after it has ceased to be appropriate or healthy. The chances that this will happen are dramatically increased with an only child because parents seem to have a more difficult time turning him loose. Their child is so very special, and he owes it to them to stay close, to maintain the integrity of the triangle. It is, unfortunately, a mind-set that almost always backfires at some point, and everybody loses. The child feels manipulated and angry, and the parents feel unappreciated and misunderstood.

Psychiatrist Selma Kramer said the only child sometimes is given a silent message by parents: "Don't relate to your peer group; stay with us. You can trust us, but you can't trust your peers." The parents may be threatened and feel abandoned if the child becomes actively involved with peers.

Kramer also said an only child who is able to ignore the silent message and go out with the peer group may be the object of a seduction attempt by one or both parents. "This girl was going to a party, and her mother told her 'If you get bored, call me and I'll bring you home. We're having a party tonight, and I'm serving your favorite pâté.' The girl was tempted to come home," and it's reasonable to assume the pâté didn't have much to do with it. She wanted to please her mother. "A lot of parents do it more subtly than this, but they do hang on more or longer when it's their only child." One result of this can be that the only child never really breaks away emotionally, but another result can be that the only child makes a greater effort to get away faster. Neither of these enhances the parent-child relationship.

What parents need to do, said Kramer, is to recognize early the strong parent-child bond and take steps to broaden the scope of the child's life by including other people. "I see parents who've never had a babysitter for their only child, and they brag about it, as if it's a sign of love and devotion. But this child is usually quite shy and retiring and doesn't know how to trust. This child has been deprived of the opportunity to learn how to deal with things when the parents go away . . . and when they come back. The frustration of the parents' leaving and the gratification of their returning are important parts of the growing-up experience, and the only child is more likely to miss this."

It's a good idea, said Kramer, for parents to "let others share in the rearing of the child—grandparents in addition to babysitters. The only child should know there are others besides parents who can give protection and security. Otherwise, the child is all tied up with the parents," and this surely is the tie that binds the only child to a relationship that inhibits growth in many ways but especially in the development of independence.

Kramer's golden rule for parents of only children: "Bring others into the act."

Psychiatrist Paul Fink put it this way: "From the day the child is born, parents should begin the process of separation. For the only child this is even more critical. Parents have to be careful to give the child enough space, to be available without being intrusive, to love without smothering." Fink said he occasionally encounters in therapy only children who are "very unhappy because the experience of being an only child has been too stressful and the pressure too great. You take a teenage girl whose mother is very intrusive when the girl's friends visit. But when she visits at a friend's house, she notices the friend's mother is kept busy with three other children, and she begins to wish she had brothers and sisters so her mother would bug out of her life."

Bringing Out the Best

A cardinal rule in parenting is to see the child as he is, not necessarily as the parents might wish him to be. What this translates to, in everyday life, is that parents need to accentuate the strengths that the child already has and play down the weaknesses. With the only child this takes on increased importance because the only child is so eternally influenced by what the parents say and do. Children with siblings have daily reality checks—"Try not to feel so bad about the way Dad put you down. He's in a crunch at work, and he's more grumpy than usual." But the only child generally has nothing with which to counterbalance parental messages on a regular basis. If Mommy and Daddy say it, it must be so, the whole truth. If the only child is told often enough that he's awkward or inept, he begins to believe it—and to act on that belief.

In the view of child psychiatrist Henri Parens, the parents of an only child "have to be careful to optimize the capabilities of the child and to accept the vulnerabilities. You try to optimize the skills and talents, but you have to be careful not to be overly demanding in areas that could undermine the child's self-esteem. . . . You take a child whose father is very sports-minded, very motor oriented. The child is sensitive, with a talent for drawing and writing. The father wants the child to be good at football, and this writing and drawing is 'sissy stuff' anyway. Clearly such a father, and there are many of them, would not be optimizing the child's magnificent skills because of his own notions of what a child should be. . . . And, of course, it works the other way, too. You take an arty family. The mother is a painter, the father a musician. The child is three years old when he finds a neighbor with a baseball bat. He swings the bat . . . and he's a natural, like Mike Schmidt. But the mother can't stand this. She doesn't like sports and all that aggression. She wants the kid to be as arty as she is, and she discourages him from playing baseball. . . . What's important here is that parents need to look at the kid and see what's there and go with that. . . . We all come into parenting with an idea of what we want. Children are quite malleable, and they become like us in many ways. They adopt our beliefs, some of our viewpoints. Kids identify with parents. It's good for us to have ideas for our children, to guide them, but we shouldn't rape their talents and skills. We shouldn't force them to become what we want them to become."

Questions and Answers, Please

The closeness that not uncommonly exists between parent and only child, at least in the early years, can become, strangely enough, a barrier to communication. A number of therapists who work with families outlined this scenario:

With an only child, parents know to a considerable extent what's going on in the child's life. As a result, parents may not ask many questions, and the child may not be confronted with the necessity to explain very much. If the child has a test, the parents know about it, and they have a sense of how the child has prepared for the test. If at day's end the child comes home with an unhappy expression, the parents pretty well can figure out what happened. Perhaps they ask "Didn't you do well?" But if the child says "I don't want to talk about it," the parents may let the matter drop. The result of this, when continued over time, is that there are few demands made on the only child to explain about himself. Contrast this, if you will, to what typically happens in a family with four or five children. There is great likelihood that the parents never knew about approaching tests and, if they did, they probably forgot about them. It then becomes each child's responsibility to explain, because parents, if they're involved, will make it a point to ask until they get what they feel is a complete answer.

While the only child tends to be highly verbal because of so much interaction with parents, he does not get to be good at explaining difficult situations. This is something that parents need to be aware of—that their only child is not developing a capacity to talk about tough things—and they need to ask him to explain and to hold him accountable. In explaining things that went wrong, the only child, in the words of one therapist, "sharpens his sense of reality. He does poorly on a test, and, because he's asked to explain, he has to come to terms with his feelings of embarrassment."

Opening the Door Wider, Beginning Real Dialogue

Psychologist Erich Coche is the father of an only child, and he was acknowledging a problem that is encountered by so many parents: how to encourage the child, especially in the teen years, to share with you what's going on in the child's world. Many only children have told me about their reluctance to share things with parents who, they feel, already are intruding too much into their lives. Coche's advice: Try to come in the back door.

"If you come head-on and say 'Tell me what's on your mind,' the child is not going to talk. You have to create the opportunity, the mood. . . . With teenagers, you probably should wait until you sense that the moment is a good one, and then you start talking. Sometimes you have to take the leadership by sharing something of your own. You set a model of faith and indicate that this is the time to exchange personal information. . . . You can say 'I'm concerned about you, about some of the things you've been saying.' A kid may drop an offhand remark. You don't have to pick it up then. You can tuck it away and bring it up later, when the time is right, when you sense that this is a good time, when the atmosphere and mood are there. It may be when you're away from the normal environment, walking on the beach, traveling in the car, camping. It's important to understand that with a teenager the parent-child relationship seems to come and go almost with wave-like motions. There will be a week or two with tension and suspicion, when the parent is seen as an enemy. Then somehow it changes, and there'll be two good weeks, with openness, willingness to listen and be friends again. The suspicion is sufficiently removed to allow openness to communication, and this is a time when a parent can share concerns.

"You can say 'Listen, a few weeks ago you said something about smoking grass at school. Can we talk about that some more?' You're coming out of a sense of concern, not heavy authority. Personally, I make the assumption that if a kid is smoking grass, he's probably unhappy about something. It's a risky assumption, but there's a high probability of being correct. I'd let the child know that I'm worried. 'If you're unhappy, will you tell me about it?' It's important that this be extended as an invitation to talk, with no force behind it."

For a long time, said Coche, parents were told that it was important to let their child know that they understood whatever the problem was at the moment. "Some parents exaggerated this and 'Oh, yes, I understand' came across to the child as a brush-off. Much of the time it may be wiser to say 'No, I don't understand. I'd like to hear more. Why are you upset? How do you feel?' Then, if the child gives you an opening and if the mood is right, go for it, ask more questions."

It's important for parents to praise the child for sharing concerns. "Let the child know that you appreciate the openness. As a parent, you are the person with authority. It's not easy for a child to be open with a parent. Everything the child says may be used against him. The child shares, and the parent says 'Hey, I've got to punish you for that.' It is risk-taking to share with parents. Let's be honest about that."

Without doubt, it takes time to communicate with the child, to create an environment that encourages sharing. But things can be postponed, temporarily. Parents can say "That's a good question, and I'm concerned, too, but I can't talk now. How about tomorrow?" The child then knows that parents are interested, if this done in a way that isn't interpreted as a brush-off. But parents have to follow up. When tomorrow comes, they've got to be available.

What Do Parents Owe Their Adult Only Child?

Parents seem to have a high degree of confusion and uncertainty about what their role is after their only child is grown. What kind of relationship is appropriate? Should they be friends or parents? That's a question that I hear from many parents. A question that I hear even more often is this: What do parents *owe* their adult child? There are no ground rules here, and parents for the most part are left to grope on their own, trying to find some middle ground where everybody will be satisfied. But sometimes this isn't possible, especially if the only child, accustomed to having so much, wants even more.

What would you do, as a parent, if your twenty-three-year-old daughter, who now is working after you paid her way through college, said that she never would speak to you again if you didn't cosign a $3,500 loan for her? It's the kind of story that I hear more frequently than you might think.

Psychiatrist Richard Moscotti said that the question should not be what do parents owe their adult children. Rather, it should be this: What do we, as parents, owe ourselves?

"I had in therapy a man who so identified with his son, who so gave of himself, that he almost became anemic from overfeeding the son. One day in therapy I asked him: 'Do you love your son enough to take good care of his father?' I really believe that we have to take care of ourselves. Parenting is one of the most difficult jobs in the world, draining, and we need time away from it, for ourselves, for our marriage. But sometimes we get lost in trying to be such wonderful parents. We want to transcend our own parents' parenting, and sometimes we overgive. . . . The love of a parent is a love that leads toward separation. Our job as parents is to try to get our child off to as good a start in life as possible to the point that the child can leave the nest at seventeen or twenty or twenty-two or whenever and cope with life. . . . I see the parenting role, at that point, as standing on the sidelines of life and pretty much staying out of the game, but being available if the adult child should fall, bleed and desperately need help."

It's important for parents of an adult child to be reasonably available, "and everybody must define what that means. Today we have twenty-five-year-old adults who get divorced and return home to cope economically. What should parents do? I think lines should be drawn, and it should be made clear that it's a temporary arrangement. 'Sally, we love you, but you can live here only for six to twelve months, and that's it.' But the trouble is that we overrespond to our guilt. We try to overcome the mistakes we made in child-rearing by doing too much after our child is grown."

What if a grown child yanks the parent's guilt chain by saying something like "If you really loved me, you would cosign my loan"? It was a question for which Moscotti seemed to be waiting. "I would say 'Look, don't try to manipulate me by playing into my guilt gland. You talk about love . . . I don't understand that. If you don't know by now that I love you, I feel you've missed the boat. I disappoint you? Well, you disappoint me by asking for too much.' If you have millions and your child owes eight thousand dollars, you might pay it off, I suppose, but you should say 'That's it. Don't ever expect it again.' And that would be it." Children aren't helped to grow up by parents who continually bail them out of trouble . . . and assume their responsibility.

In his office, Moscotti has a sign that reads HOW ABOUT THAT? It's an important message for parents to consider, he said. "Your child says he's disappointed in you as a father. Well, how about that? Sometimes to force children to grow up, we are required to take a hard line, with drill-sergeantlike rigidity. Eventually the little bird must learn to fly on its own."

The Problem of Affluence

People with plenty of money, mostly those who earned it, tend to have a special problem as parents, and the problem, in the view of Spurgeon English, is that they tend to shortchange their child. Oh, yes, they give the child everything that money can buy, but they so often don't give the child those most precious of all gifts: their time and attention.

"We find families in which there is economic comfort and concern for the child's education in the best schools and material things that are supposed to bring happiness to the young. Yet the child grows up to battle anxiety, depression and fears of life's many changing events" to a degree that suggests that the economically privileged child may be in worse shape than the child who has grown up in much more modest circumstances. "The child of the privileged often ultimately receives disappointment in receiving the essential help in growing up enjoyably. The privileged people seem to accept their success and enjoy it, but they don't include their child among the ingredients for their success and enjoyment of life. They seem to consider their child often to be a burden and source of problems rather than a contributing part of the parents' daily life. Happiness, instead, is expressed by the parents at a party with contemporaries or on a vacation with their peers after they have made conscientious efforts to obtain adequate babysitters or companions for the child's care while they are living the good life."

The problem, said English, is that these parents seem to place a "sharp division between their achievement and their parenthood. . . . They may feel it is a badge of success and social altruism to have a child, but they find it difficult to grow with and share themselves with the child." They may transmit to their child the message that the child's worth is to be found in achievement rather than in mere existence. Because of lack of much input by anybody but parents, the only child needs especially to be told and shown that he "can sit on the floor or run around the room and be a source of satisfaction" to parents without performing or achieving. The child who doesn't get this message rather consistently grows up with low self-esteem and without a sense of importance.

"There's something about financial achievement that hardens the mind," said English, and causes many materially successful people to become lonely and isolated and to attach a dollar sign to everything they do. "I don't hear too many financially successful men talk about their time with the child, about hugging, praising, sharing—the things that give self-esteem to the child. The father waits until the boy can play golf with him" before he wants to get to know the boy and spend much time with him. "The father doesn't think the little boy is worth much time or effort. How can the father give up his time, which is worth two hundred dollars an hour, to play with a five-year-old? So he doesn't do it and then it may be too late. The son may not want to play golf, may not accept the father's friendship. A child needs interest more when he's younger, not older. If parents don't show interest when the child is young, the child won't trust the show of interest later when parents say how proud they are of the law degree or graduation from medical school. That's when the child may ask 'Where were you when I was eight?' To show appreciation you have got to spend time together, do things together."

Does this mean that the hard-charging, two hundred dollar-an-hour father may have to back off some from his career? Yes, said English, that's exactly what it means. "This is a very hard concept to sell to fathers."

12

Marrying the Only Child

"When I married him, I thought he was introspective and sensitive. Now I realize that he's just spoiled. He expects me to cater to him just like his mother did." That's what one woman who married an only child told me.

"She still thinks she's Daddy's little girl, and if I don't measure up to Daddy, which I usually don't, she always reminds me that I'm not meeting her needs." That's what one man who married an only child told me.

Fact or fiction? Is this what it's *really* like to be married to an only child. Is he or she a narcissistic demon whose self-centeredness exceeds the bounds of reality? Or is the only child in marriage pretty much like anybody else, if you cast aside the stereotypes and focus instead on the person?

The answer, it seems to me, is a little bit of both. The only child does tend to have some special qualities that call for special understanding by the spouse. But the only child is not necessarily a difficult person to live with. If it seems otherwise, it's probably because normal rough spots that come up in all marriages tend so often to be blamed on the only child, who is forever pinned with the label of being selfish and spoiled. This is a myth, said psychiatrist Martin Goldberg, director of the Marriage Council of Philadelphia, which trains marital therapists. "I don't see any more selfishness in marriages involving only children than in other marriages. Selfishness has to do not with being an only child but with how you were raised. Just as often, it's the last child, the baby in the family, who is spoiled and selfish. Enough things happen in life to make you either sharing or selfish, and it has not much to do with being an only child. But if you're an only child, you'll be accused of being selfish. You can count on that. It's a stock accusation in marital arguments," red-hot ammunition for the spouse to fire at the adult only child.

Do adult only children get divorced more often than persons with siblings? No, there is no evidence to support this. The formal studies that have been done tend to be inconclusive. What about only children in unhappy marriages that, for whatever reasons, never end in divorce? Are only children disproportionately represented in these unhappy marriages? No, that doesn't seem to be the case. Marital therapists have told me over and over that only children are not overrepresented in the client population.

So what does it all mean? When an only child gets married, what are the special problems that can surface? Let me share with you the thoughts of some experienced therapists.

Martin Goldberg: "One thing I see with some frequency is that the only child, after marriage, has to adjust to the process of sharing. That there is another main actor in the play is something that is new to the only child, who is accustomed to being the one and only star. It takes more of an adjustment for the only child to become part of a duo. What can the spouse do? Be aware that it's natural for an only child to be like this. The spouse shouldn't immediately make demands or push too fast. Often the spouse compounds the difficulty of the adjustment by saying 'You're spoiled rotten,' but, as I have said, this has nothing to do with being an only child.

"If you compare only children to children from large families, you find that only children have less tendency to share their thoughts and feelings. This is because, as they were growing up, they didn't have such easy access to somebody to listen to them. With siblings, you have more people to listen, and you potentially get more practice. It's important for the spouse to understand that it may take an only child longer to make this adjustment" and to become able to share as freely as the spouse would like.

What happens when an only child marries an only child? "There were some battles royal, based on the few cases I can recall. They were highly individualistic people in the best and worst sense, and they had many clashes. Only children do tend to be more individualistic. Their individualism doesn't get sanded down by relationships with siblings." To the extent that two highly individualistic people are prone to have more problems than two people who are less individualistic, it would be reasonable to assume that only children who marry only children can expect some additional conflict.

What if the marriage ends? How does an adult only child tend to handle divorce? "My guess is that only children have a greater fear of abandonment than children from large families. The smaller the family, the more frightened a person is by the prospect of loss. I would say that, on average, divorce is tougher for an [adult] only child because the fear of abandonment is stronger."

Psychiatrist Selma Kramer: "As adults, only children may have trouble dealing with authority. In growing up, they had their parents as authority figures, and they had lots of attention from their parents. As adults, they may expect other authority figures to give them attention, too, to give them the same credit for their prowess as they got from their parents. If the boss, for instance, doesn't give the only child credit for being exceptional, the only child may regard the boss as a real SOB, without considering the reasons why. The only child has a need to be regarded as special, not only by the boss but also by the spouse. This is something that the spouse needs to understand and prepare for. . . . The spouse also needs to be prepared for a certain degree of self-centeredness, based not on nastiness but on experience. But this doesn't mean that they can't work things out in the husband-wife relationship."

Psychologist Carol Gantman: "There has been a lot written about self-centeredness and only children. To some extent we're all self-centered. We view ourselves as the center of the world, and there's some need for that. 'My needs have priority.' A healthy degree of self-centeredness is necessary to survive. We have to make it clear that we're talking about 'When I need care for me instead of you.' The border of selfishness is invaded when decisions about what should be done are made only in light of what is good for me, without any concern for you. 'No matter what you think, I'll do it anyway.' It's like the border between being assertive and being aggressive. It comes down to impacting negatively on other people to get what you want for yourself. The potential is greater for this with an only child" because of the way his or her life has been scripted. But the spouse needs to recognize that "what looks like selfishness may in reality be a preoccupation with self, with no malice. It's just that the other person didn't consider the impact on you." Understanding and communication are helpful.

Psychiatrist Pirooz Sholevar: "The only child, accustomed to being at the center of attention, has difficulty with separating benign neglect from hostile neglect. You pick up a book and read for two hours, and the only child who is your spouse may see this as your ignoring him or being mad at him. It's a difference in perception. You see yourself as doing your own thing; the only child sees it as an unfriendly act."

The only child can feel overly entitled to the good things of life—and be overly demanding. That's bad enough when the good things come from the parents while the only child is growing up. It's worse when the spouse is expected to continue giving the good things. "A wife came to me for counseling because she was depressed. Her complaint was that her husband didn't love her anymore. I asked why she thought that, and she said that he didn't bring her roses every week like he used to. She was an only child and her expectation was that she would get gifts weekly. Her husband, in the beginning, had vowed always to show his appreciation of her, and they had what was almost a princess-slave relationship. It continued until the husband ran up so many debts that he was forced to stop buying gifts. . . . A problem I see with only children is that, because they were admired by their parents, they feel that the spouse's job is to admire them, too. If they're not admired, they may think that they are not loved."

Psychiatrist Henri Parens: "I would suggest that the spouse be aware that, in stressful times, the only child may become more narcissistic. Under stress, the only child may be more demanding, may expect to be treated as a prince or princess. The spouse should try to help the only child by being supportive and loving and must be careful not to attack the narcissistic expression of stress. To attack the narcissism can only intensify the stress and the feeling of impoverished self-esteem. . . . It's important for the spouse not to respond in kind, even though it's a natural thing to do. When we're stressed and feeling hostile, we may go for areas of vulnerability in the other person. We're all tempted to do it at times, but in marriage we have to be especially careful not to do it. Even the vicious sport of boxing has rules. You don't hit below the belt. But married people tend to disregard the rules. They hit below the belt by going for the vulnerability in the other person."

In other words, they're dirty fighters.

When Love Becomes War

Years ago, psychologist George Bach coined the term "intimate enemies" to describe those with whom we are cozy but sometimes clash—our spouses, sweethearts, children, parents, special friends. Bach's position was that it's not only inevitable but also healthy for us to cross swords with these people because "real intimacy demands that there be fighting. . . . Nonfighting is only appropriate between strangers—people who have nothing worth fighting about. When two people begin to really care about each other, they become emotionally vulnerable, and the battles start."

But the trouble with these battles, from Bach's perspective, is that they don't do what "good" battles should do: clear the air and pave the way for understanding and acceptance. The underlying reason for this is that many of us are dirty fighters and we muck up things, because it's more important for us to win than to resolve our problems fairly. Everywhere he looked, Bach once told me in an interview, he found dirty fighters. It was enough to make him want to start a marital-fight center to help people learn to fight more productively.

Dirty fighting is a problem that many therapists encounter regularly in their work with couples. Until couples learn to fight fairly, they're never going to resolve their underlying difficulties, because they're battling not about issues but about symptoms. I asked psychiatrist Alan Summers why there seemingly are so many dirty fighters. What is the payoff?

"You have a sense of guiltlessness, of self-righteousness, because you project all of the blame on the other person. The problems were started by the other person, and so you take no responsibilities." Almost always the other person is put on the defensive—to try to ward off the below-the-belt punches. Summers said that in his career he has seen some classic techniques of dirty fighting, including these:

· *Playing psychiatrist.* This gives the dirty fighter "a sense of control, an advantage. 'The reason you're doing this is . . .' and there can be as many reasons as there are people. A woman might say to a man 'You're a mama's boy' or 'You've been castrated.' A man might say to a woman 'You're a gold-digger' or 'You're still in love with your father.' The idea is for the dirty fighter to intimidate the other person into accepting the blame."

· *Using the children as weapons.* The wife says to the husband "The reason Johnny skips school is that you're never home to be his father." The husband says to the wife "Our kids are in trouble because you overprotect them and never hold them accountable for anything."

· *Using sex as a weapon.* The woman has a headache, said Summers, "because she feels that she's not getting what she wants, which can be anything from a fur coat to the husband's attention. . . . Men refuse to have sex with their wives, too. We tend to think of men as always being hungry for sex, but men can turn off sex when they want to punish their wives. They withhold closeness, which insults women's femininity. The message is 'You're not attractive to me'—which denies the cosmetic appeal that women are raised to have."

· *Attacking rather than acknowledging feelings.* The man says to the woman "You're lazy and no good; you don't take care of our children." What he really means is "I need more attention; I'm feeling insecure."

· *Playing hurtful games.* The woman says "If it hadn't been for you, I could have married that successful lawyer." The man says "I could have taken that big promotion to Chicago, but, no, you had to stay near your mother."

Where do people learn to be dirty fighters? Probably from parents who were dirty fighters, too, said Summers. "They come from a point of basic mistrust," and they don't feel good about themselves. It's likely that all of us, no matter how healthy we are, will slip occasionally and resort to dirty fighting, but people who consistently fight dirty are running scared—and they need help. Help from whom? From the targets of their attacks, from the intimate enemies who love the dirty fighters enough to help them.

"You have to be able to acknowledge and tend to the dirty fighter's vulnerability. The dirty fighter attacks you out of his own sense of vulnerability. He fights dirty when he feels insecure, unloved, unneeded, out of control. You have to try to give him what he needs and to share some of your own vulnerabilities. This is hard to do when you're under siege. It's next to impossible, but there's really no other way." Example: The husband says to his dirty-fighting wife: "It looks as if you feel that you don't get enough respect and recognition for your efforts." If the man can acknowledge this much, he is saying that he's going to see what he can do to make things better. This helps the woman's feelings of not being appreciated and is a step toward unplugging her from her need to hit below the belt.

Some other things that can be helpful to adult only children in ending dirty fighting in their intimate relationships:

Agree to use "I" statements, which explain how you feel about something, rather than "you" statements, which blame the other person. Example: "I feel unloved when the house isn't kept clean" as opposed to "If you weren't so lazy, the house wouldn't be this filthy."

Pretend that the past never happened. In Summer's words, "concentrate on what you're going to do in the future, rather than on what's already taken place. This way you wipe out the idea that the problem exists because of what the other person did."

More Realism, Please

Because the only child, in the growing-up years at home, became accustomed to having the world pretty much his way, he has difficulty accepting that in marriage he can't always have what he wants, that he can't order away the bad times, that he must be more realistic. In the words of psychologist Moss Jackson, "You can accept that at times the relationship will be good, at times not so good and even bad. There will be highs and lows. You can accept that the other person is not ideal," but a real flesh-and-blood human who, like the only child, has warts, a nasty temper and gloomy days as well as beauty, charm and optimism.

The marriages that work best and last longest, in Jackson's opinion, are those that are flavored with intimacy and communication. This doesn't just happen. It is the result of determination and effort, two items that didn't necessarily get called for very often in the only child's early years. "In a long-term relationship that works, what prevails is the feeling of 'I'm interested in your welfare.' You can't be intensely romantic all the time, but you can maintain an active interest in each other." It's important for the couple to appreciate the relationship as a haven to which they can retreat and be themselves. This, perhaps, is the ultimate definition of a successful marriage. "They know that they don't have to treat each other as they were treated in the outside world. They don't have to make up for what they didn't get out in the world. The relationship is a place where they can let their guard down and be cared for."

What about an only child who is well cared for—even idolized—in the outside world? Does he expect that treatment and only that treatment at home from the spouse?

For twelve years Monica, one of four children, has been married to Jeffrey, an only child, active in community affairs, respected as a trial lawyer. At times Monica feels that she is expected to be an endless source of nurturing "because that's what he gets so much of from everybody else, from the world. They think the guy walks on water, and when I treat him as my husband, he thinks I'm mad at him and don't appreciate him. I'm the only person in the world, I think, who stands up to him, and he regards that as criticism. He hates criticism . . . he loves praise. Hell, so do I, but I don't expect to be praised all the time. I feel that my tank is running empty. I can't keep giving and giving, but that's what he expects."

Jeffrey's view is decidedly different. "I am very good at what I do for a living. People respect that. I'm also a decent person, easy enough to get along with, and people like that. Home is the only place where I constantly have to defend myself. She's upset because her career is not as far along as mine, and she takes her frustration out on me by being critical, by trying to tear me down. I know I don't walk on water." At that point, Jeffrey paused, smiled cheerfully and added: "But I'm a great swimmer!"

In marriage the only child probably needs more space, because, in growing up, he typically had more space than children with siblings. He spent a good bit of time alone; nobody barged unannounced into his room; his little universe provided what he needed. The best marriages, said Moss Jackson, offer "enough" space, and how much is enough is determined by the partners themselves.

"At times we need space. We need to be alone. At these times, when I need to be alone, if you need my presence to reaffirm that I love you, I can't do it," and hurt feelings are likely to result. "But if you have a sense of yourself, that you're lovable, if you don't think that I always have to be with you to prove it, then you can give me space. To get more intimacy, we may have to give each other more space." People need "a sense of their own autonomy. 'I am a separate person. Even if you leave, I'll still exist.' But if I define myself by how much you tell me that you care for me, then I'm in a trap. If you don't tell me, I don't feel loved."

When does space become a negative force? If there's too much space, if people always go their separate ways, doesn't the marriage at some point begin to resemble not a marriage but an arrangement, an occasional coming together of roommates? Jackson's opinion is that space becomes negative when it robs the relationship of passion and communication. "If you don't have that, the interest in each other, then you have a marriage of convenience. You've lost the art of staying involved and helping each other on the quest. You have to promote the other person's discovery and be excited about it. This enhances your own quest."

First, There's His Problem . . .

The man's problem—and, like so many other things, it's exaggerated if he's an only child—is that he doesn't know how to show his vulnerability. It's hard for him to cry when he's hurt and to bleed when he's wounded, and this is what clamps a stranglehold on many men as they try to be good-enough husbands. If they don't know and appreciate themselves, how can they know and appreciate their wives? Victor Gruhn, a retired Lutheran pastor, put it this way: "We have to be wounded to achieve our humanity because in the sterility of the technology of the world in which we live, we don't have to show love. We can marry our jobs."

Fathers try to "stamp out anything feminine in male children. They don't do it necessarily by saying 'Don't act like a girl.' I don't remember that my father ever said that. But the things that a father encourages are pulled up in importance. . . . There wasn't much money in our family during the Depression, but my father always had money for me to see a historical movie that he thought was worthwhile. I was encouraged to learn, achieve, get ahead. That's where the focus was. . . . The last thing my mother said to me was 'Oh, your father would be so proud of you now.' And she was glowing. But she wasn't talking about my love, only about achievement. . . . Because men are attracted to achievement, their whole world can be wrapped up in their work," and they can become experts at denying anything, such as emotion, that threatens their rush toward achievement. "I grew up on self-denial," said Gruhn, "and I'm still trying to bring myself out of it, to get out of the austere world and go for myself, to realize that I've neglected myself and starved myself out of a lot of things. I used to carry in my pocket one piece of a jigsaw puzzle. I called it that part of me that's missing, that part of me that I can't find alone, my humanity, compassion and love. I need other people to help me find it."

How can we men find the missing part? By accepting the equality of the person who means the most to us, our wives. We can do it by letting her help us, said Gruhn. "But the trouble is that we tend to see the woman not as a person. To be a real person, after all, you must be a male. We all know that, don't we? So we protect her; we do all the nice things for her, except give her full personhood. But what we don't see is that by enabling her to grow, we do something about fullness for ourselves. We can't do it alone, but the stupidity of the John Wayne syndrome gets in the way, and we think that we can do it by ourselves. . . . We can change our lives just as alcoholics change their lives, by hitting bottom and then starting the long climb back. We hit bottom when we realize that we need help, her help. We can begin to change when we recognize a woman as a person equal to ourselves. She is a person; it's OK for me to accept an idea from her; it's OK to appreciate that she has a brain, too."

Then There Is Her Problem . . .

Because achievement is so important to only children, female as well as male, problems that arise in marriage and even in dating can have their roots in a tunnel-vision drive to succeed in the workplace. But the price for success can be different for the woman than for the man. While the man may burn out emotionally or break down physically, the woman tends to struggle with relationships that wither and turn brown or that never even get off the ground. Psychologist Judith Sills, author of *How to Stop Looking for Someone Perfect and Find Someone to Love,* said it's beyond doubt that career women do have some special problems with men.

"If they're very successful, if they earn more than the man, if they hold a higher position, they have a divorce rate that's higher" than the average for all women. In their divorces these women tend to be the ones "who get left. They do not do the leaving." The men leave because they have great difficulty in dealing with women who shoot for the moon and hit it dead center. But, said Sills, a lot of what happens hinges on how the woman feels about herself. If she's happily married and then goes on to establish herself as a success, she tends to get so much support from the outside world that she asks less of her marriage. She's more comfortable. She understands how the world works, and she probably appreciates her husband more" because she values him for who he is, rather than for what he represents. This is the kind of woman who, if she is divorced or widowed, can "marry the chauffeur and feel OK about it because she doesn't have to prove a point to anybody."

The career women who have the most difficulty in sustaining relationships with men, said Sills, are those who are still climbing the ladder, not the relatively few who already are at or near the top. "I'm talking about the woman who is twenty-five to thirty-four, making $35,000 or so. She's worked five or ten years and can't decide on her next career move. She's very attractive, well-dressed, regularly goes to the health club to exercise. There are a hundred thousand of these women for every one who has really succeeded. This is the woman who has trouble with her list of demands" regarding men with whom she could get serious. "She is looking for somebody perfect, but she puts the blame for not finding anybody on men, rather than on herself. She is reluctant to make a commitment because 'men are strange. They stop calling if you go to bed with them, and they stop calling if you don't go to bed with them.' This woman can walk into a room with nine men in it and immediately call a girlfriend and say that nobody was acceptable. They didn't look right or didn't dress right. But then she's depressed because she doesn't have a relationship."

What tends to hang this woman up, in Sills's words, is that she "is looking for a new life and it has to be better than the life she's made for herself. She's more important than any man and she wants to stay that way. If she gets married, it must be to somebody who won't drag her down to his level. With this attitude is it any wonder that she's lonely, bitter and frustrated? She has to let herself love a nice guy and not feel she's done it out of desperation. If she can't do that, she's going to be all alone. She is the Cinderella girl who grows up, and in the process loses self-esteem. She can't understand why she's not in a relationship. She thought by twenty-eight she'd be starting a family, but now she doesn't know where the last eight years went. In bed at night, alone, she feels hopeless. So many women have said to me 'If I thought I'd have to live like this forever, I'd kill myself.' I think all she has to do is change her attitude." What she and married career women, too, must guard against is getting so wrapped up in their work and in themselves that they lose the capacity to value other people, the ability to treasure the positive qualities even as they acknowledge the negatives.

Ah, yes, career women who are so wrapped in their work. That's a problem, too, for the men in their lives.

And, Finally, There Is Their Problem

In the old days—whether they were good or bad was in the eye of the beholder—the man ruled the roost. Said psychiatrist John Reckless: "He dictated at work, and when he came home to his 'traditional' wife, what he said was the way it was. She stroked his ego and made him feel good, although he probably never recognized many of the things that she did to support him." Their marriage sailed along—as good as anybody else's, it seemed—although at times she felt that he regarded home as a kind of service station, where he paused for clean shirts, socks and emotional regeneration before flying off to slay the next dragon. If they argued, which they seldom did, the man "felt that his wife was a two-pound bird in a one-pound nest with her mouth open saying 'more.' When she talked, he heard 'money.' But what she was saying was 'give me time and talk with me.' "

Yes, that's how it was in the old days, so long ago and so far away. . . .

In his current practice, Dr. Reckless deals often with the crumbling mortar of marriage, especially two-career marriage. A primary problem with these marriages today, he said, is caused by role reversal. The woman, in the man's view, is using home as a service station, and he doesn't like it. But what is he doing about it? Not much, and that's at the core of the problem. The man is sitting back, muffling his anger, withdrawing and wondering what happened to "the wonderful girl I married."

In times past the man didn't have to deal with a wife who wanted to negotiate an equal relationship. Now the man is "torn between intellectually agreeing with equality and emotionally disagreeing" with what he perceives equality is taking away from him—the tender, loving care for which this wife no longer has time because she must be in New York on Monday and in Dallas on Tuesday. The husband's response is to burn with anger, but he can't deal angrily with her because he's conditioned by society and mother not to hurt the woman he loves. So, said Reckless, "the man pulls back, nurses his wounds, becomes emotionally passive. That's what we're seeing today—more men who are more emotionally passive. In the old days the wife would have time to talk and take the initiative, but now she's at the office or on the road, and there's no time to help the husband deal with his hurt. Off she goes for three days, and the things he's accustomed to are not there. He doesn't realize fully the extent of his anger, because it's buried, and so he deals with it indirectly—by withholding information from her, by trying to fill the niche with an affair, with alcohol or with drugs."

But, I asked Reckless, wasn't the commitment to two careers and everything that this implies discussed by these two people before marriage? Yes, he said, but there's a wide gap between projecting how it's going to be and discovering how it really is. "The man she chose to marry was on the way up, a man of similar philosophy about equal rights for women. He was supportive, willing to share, do his tasks. He was not the enemy. He was the enabler who helped her make the transition to professional life." But then something happened. "As she succeeded, she was recognized and promoted to a fast track. She no longer was an invisible person. She now was recognized for her intellect, and, make no mistake, it's an ego trip for her. Her income goes up, equal to or beyond his, and the man has trouble with the competition. They work on their tax returns, and he says to her, 'I'll get you next year.' He begins to pull away, and their sexual relationship fades." He feels angry; she feels slighted and wonders what happened to "the nice guy I married."

Reckless said power is "an aphrodisiac for women. . . . So now she's at the New York meeting in the boardroom, and she's looking at the big man. This guy has no need to put a move on an employee and risk a lawsuit. His viewpoint is that she's an exciting person and 'I can learn from her.' She makes her presentation. He knows that she has four hours before she catches her plane to Dallas, and he asks her to go to dinner with him. She's wondering 'How can this be happening to me? A year ago I was a teller, and now I'm at dinner with the chairman of the board.' You put a man and woman together in a business situation—with sharing, time together in a relaxed atmosphere—and . . . well, they enjoy each other. She can talk to him. It's not a genital kind of sexuality, but it's definitely a kind of sexuality. They want to continue the relationship, which is quite innocent. On the plane trip to Dallas, she thinks about the man back home, the man who has withdrawn and become so lacking in assertiveness. She begins to question if this is the man for her. No, she decides, he's probably not the man for her."

I asked Reckless if this really happens. His answer: "I see forty or fifty cases a year like this."

What's the answer? Quite simply, the answer is for the man to assert himself, said Reckless, to insist that the wife pay some attention to him and weigh her career in relation to their marriage. What makes his being assertive so difficult is that the man first must come face to face with his "unacceptable" anger, and typically this happens only when he feels that he has been given permission to feel it. Who can grant this permission? Other men in the same boat, and that's the powerful benefit that can be gained from group therapy.

"What I'm talking about is male bonding, one man getting together with another man with an agenda. 'I'm unhappy; can I come over tonight and talk?' A man can do this if he's developed a network of friends," and through this network he becomes better able to deal assertively with his wife, to ask for what he wants. How does the wife react to this new assertiveness? "If a man lets a woman walk on him, she has no respect for him. But if he becomes emotionally assertive—'This is a marriage, not a business arrangement. I need your time. Do you have to go on so many trips?'—then there's something in the woman that causes her to pay attention. . . . A woman will give an ultimatum to a man who's a patsy but not to a strong man. She picks up that he's changing—he's able to express anger and then good feelings follow—and she thinks 'I've been taking him for granted. If I don't get my act together, I'm going to lose him.' And maybe she then finds it's possible to rearrange some of the travel so she's not gone so much."

What happens to the woman's career? "Corporations are becoming aware that they have to be more humanistic, have to be good to their good people to keep them." On some level, said Reckless, many women seem to be aware, if their men remind them, that giving everything to a career is a long road to hard times. "They've heard about the women who at fifty-five wake up at the top of the tree, lonely, with a network of female friends like themselves, and wonder what went wrong. Like men, they ask 'Was it worth it?' And, like men, they usually answer 'No, there has to be more to life than this.' "

Even only children who are driven to acheive can understand this, and they, men and women alike, can correct their life courses—while there's still time. That's the happy script for this story, but sometimes, unfortunately, this is not the way it the story ends.

What About the Money?

Psychologist Thelma Shtasel posed this question: Why is it that so many husbands flinch and fall back if their wives prosper "too much" in their careers? She answered her own question: The reason most commonly given is money. The man feels emasculated, diminished and discounted if he's not the primary breadwinner. But money is a convenient peg on which to hang discontent—not the real reason. "It's easier for a man to say that he feels bad because she makes more money, easier than saying that he feels bad because she has more prestige. Often that's the real reason—more prestige."

An example from Shtasel's casebook: "The man is a physician, but he doesn't especially like being a physician. He makes a lot of money but not as much as he could. He takes a lot of time off, plays golf four times a week. His wife started a little business, and it really took off. Now she employs a dozen people, and she's earning more than he. He's very upset," but the reason for the upset, when the underbrush is cut away, is that "she's known as a businesswoman. She goes to business meetings, to conventions. She's no longer 'the doctor's wife.' He's the businesswoman's husband, and he's more threatened by that. She's better known. I think money has nothing to do with it."

This is not an uncommon reaction among men who don't feel good about themselves and their careers. "I know another man whose wife earns more and is better known, and he told me: 'A problem? I love it. I'm successful. Why should I care?' That seems to be the difference—if a man feels that he's successful by his standard and by the standards of his family and friends. The dollar is not nearly so important to him as to the guy who feels that he's not made it. . . . It's what the money stands for. What is the money symbolic of—that she's a success and he's a failure? Or that he's a failure, period? Sometimes he is a failure, but a lot of times he's not," and good therapy can help him reshape his perception of himself and his career. "The wife may be in a field that pays more. He's a teacher, and a teacher is not going to make as much as an accountant, usually. So, in therapy, I'd try to help the man shift his view. They both can enjoy the money, if it's a good marriage." What about prestige? "I'd ask the man to reevaluate himself in terms of his own goals. Does he feel good about himself? If not, why not? Could he do better at his own job—or is he slipping below his capacity because he's more concerned about his wife?"

Shtasel said that it's not uncommon for marriages to fail because husbands and wives disagree on the importance of careers. "You take two professionals who are married, and maybe the man wants to be on a slower track. He's willing to earn $40,000, but she wants a faster track. She wants more. So in a while she's making $60,000, and he's still at $40,000. She's working twelve hours a day; he's working eight. He wants to spend evenings with her, but she's always at meetings. I can see a divorce coming out of this. He may marry another professional, but it'll be a woman whose priority, like his, is to spend time at home together."

The Wife Who Is a Pleaser

A girl who grows up without a reasonably close relationship with her father tends to carry a faulty self-image and to suffer from what therapists call "father hunger." She doesn't feel pretty, and she spends a big part of her life trying to please the man to whom she is married. She'll do anything in the world for this man, but the trouble is that she makes bad choices in men because the choices are based on finding somebody to please.

Psychologist Kevin Leman has a name for these woman—"pleasers"—and he wrote a book about them: *The Pleasers: Women Who Can't Say No—and the Men Who Control Them.* The woman who is destined to become a pleaser, said Leman, often is the first-born daughter or, especially, the only daughter, "who could be a super pleaser. She wants the ocean of life to be smooth, and she has a very difficult time saying no. She seeks approval. Many of the pleasers are 'Martha Luthers,' women who try to be great reformers. They take on men as reclamation projects."

Leman told me that the father is a dominant figure in the life of a daughter who becomes a pleaser. "We always hear about mother-daughter relationships, but the cross-sexual relationship is really critical. So many women have told me that when the father just looked at them, they shaped up. They could be a little girl around mother, but with father they tried to be perfect."

This hunger for father's approval is what sets the woman up to spend a lifetime trying to win male approval. "A cake falls flat without a major ingredient," said Leman, "and a woman falls flat without the right masculine influence," which provides love, support and acceptance.

When the Grass Looks Greener

Sometimes the only child who is brought up in relative isolation brings into a marriage a burden that impacts heavily on the spouse. Roger's story is a classic example. His father often traveled on business, and his mother was "very independent and out of the house a good deal of the time. . . . I was left alone, to my own resources, and loneliness was the basic experience of my growing-up years. My personality was formed around growing up lonely."

Now forty-five and a medical doctor in the Midwest, Roger said the lack of contact with other people caused him to "generate certain fantasies about what sex was supposed to be, what relationships were supposed to give you. Everything became exaggerated in importance because in these fantasies everything was so idealized. Relationships and intimacy seemed to be the answers to everything for me," yet because he constantly sought perfection in relationships, he always felt disappointed, and this unquestionably was a factor in two divorces and the demise of more relationships than he wants to remember.

"When a relationship doesn't live up to my expectations, I feel deprived, and this puts my partner in a position of being inadequate to meet my needs. Momentarily, I've been able to get satisfaction in relationships, but it doesn't last. My fantasies always run ahead of reality. An overriding theme in my life is a sense of being deprived, because nobody can give me the perfect relationship. The grass always looks greener in another relationship; some other relationship always seems more promising. 'Why should I stick in this relationship when I'm in such a deprived state?' And then I'm scanning the horizon for something better. This makes it extremely difficult on the other person. If she wasn't paranoid before, something like this can make her paranoid."

Getting the Help You Need from Your Spouse

Is it possible for the spouse to help the only child heal the wounds from childhood, to supply some of what the only child didn't get earlier or to modify some of what the only child got too much of? Yes, said psychologist Herb Cohen, though it's very much a two-way street. In a mature marriage spouses can help each other and, in a way, can become therapists to each other. "In my work with couples I've found that it is possible to teach them to be the benevolent parent to each other that they lacked in growing up. Through this type of relationship, each partner can begin to be healed of their very early hurts and disappointments."

What can couples do? "Talk with each other about what childhood was like, what you liked and didn't like, what you got enough of and didn't get enough of, what was valuable and what was not. . . . You can pick out things you felt were absent when you were growing up and talk in depth about these things. You can begin to acknowledge some of the deficits, and you can see if the partner can give you enough" of what was missing. For this to be successful, couples must have "a certain openness, a willingness to look at themselves, to share with each other, the ability to hear each other."

Here is one story from Cohen's files: "This man grew up in a family where the father was peripheral. The mother worked, and the man grew up relatively alone and undisciplined. Now he was married, and he was gambling a lot. When he and his wife came to see me, lack of discipline was not the presenting problem.

Gambling was the problem. . . . I assisted the wife in becoming the disciplining father to the husband and, over time, she became like the father he never had. With my help the man responded to it . . . and began to see that his acting out in an immature way—by his gambling—was his way of saying 'I need limits set for me.' The wife got a sense of power and strength that she'd never felt before, and the husband began to internalize the discipline that he never had."

These people, said Cohen, were about the same age, but it's apparent to him that age really has nothing to do with the roles that partners can assume in helping each other. Cohen, who is forty, said that in therapy he had "become a father" to a sixty-seven-year-old man who is a client. "His father died when he was four, and he was raised by his mother. He had no masculine identity. He has become able to see me as a kind of surrogate father, and I see him as a needy boy inside a sixty-seven-year-old body. We've been involved for two years, and the context for this was created when he was able to regress and be a needy little boy who needed to be fathered. At times he's even called me 'Daddy.' He plays with that in a joking way, but it's important to him. As a result of what has happened, he's better able to be a father to his own son."

How can couples help each other? "You take a wife who feels that her father never had enough time for her. Maybe the husband could make it a point regularly to do something special just for her, to heal some of the hurts from her not feeling special. Maybe the wife was not encouraged by her parents to go into the work world and make a mark. The husband can be her cheerleader, like a benevolent mother who could encourage her daughter. . . . Maybe the husband has just been turned down for a job. The wife can be understanding and can affirm his ability to be out in the world. That's what a parent does for a while. 'I know you can do it.' Am I talking just about mutual support? That's part of it, but there's something about making it explicit, about promoting and encouraging parent-child interaction, about hearing some of the hurts and disappointments that we felt in growing up."

What most people need most is to feel understood. "If they feel understood by others, it opens incredible doors to be willing to take in love from others. Above all else, couples want to be known to each other, to be understood." What if one partner wants more love than the other partner can give? "If parenting deficiencies were so extreme, you're never going to fill up for what was missed. But you can get some. You can get more than you ever had before. You can begin to fill in some of the cracks in your foundation and begin to identify yourself not as incomplete and insufficient but as incomplete and getting better, getting more of what you need to be healthy."

Clara is married to Frank, who is an only child, and I would like to believe she speaks for many spouses who are married to only children: "At times he can be self-righteous as hell, but underneath it all, he's the nicest fellow you would want to meet. He's sensitive and ambitious and loving. Every woman should have it this good."

I like the sound of that, don't you?

Epilogue

The handwriting is unmistakably boyish—loose, looping letters that form words that ride precariously atop the pale blue lines of the two-ring orange-and-black notebook paper. The paper is smudged with fingerprints, and some of the holes along the margin are ripped out, so that the pages sometimes slide out of the notebook, the back cover of which is hanging on by a few fragile strands of thread.

One of the short stories in the notebook is entitled "Itching Fingers," and it begins this way:

Slim Dalton, ace gambler of Dodge City, was seated at a gambling table at a saloon. He and three other rough-looking men were gambling. Slim was dealing the cards, and quickly he dealt two cards from the bottom of the deck. One of the ruffians saw Slim do it and said "OK, Slim, I wouldn't do that!" Slim's face was getting red. At last he shouted "What are you going to do about it?" The ruffian answered "This!"—and quickly drew for his gun. But Slim, the fastest gun-drawer in Dodge City, was too fast. His gun rang out, and smoke filled the room. The ruffian dropped his gun and fell heavily to the floor.

Quickly, the two other men drew for their guns, but Dalton, seeing that the odds were against him, fled for the steps.

The other men followed after him. Turning and firing, Slim let another one of his slugs enter one of the men, who immediately fell backward. By that time the other men from the saloon were after Dalton. They had him cornered in a lone room at the dark end of the hall. Just then a tall stranger entered the saloon. He was dressed in black. His name was Ken Maynard. . . .

As you leaf cautiously through the notebook, you find other stories that reflect the interests of a ten-year-old Midwestern boy—stories about cowboys and baseball players, and about fighter pilots, sailors and foot soldiers, who were heroic-beyond-belief figures of the times. This, you see, was 1942, and it was at the beginning of the war to end all wars, to save democracy and make the world safe for everybody's children and grandchildren.

The ten-year-old boy who wrote the stories knew beyond question what he wanted to do with his life. He would be a writer, and he never would consider anything else. The sounds of words fascinated him, and stringing together words to create a thought or paint a picture were as much fun, almost, as listening to the radio broadcasts of his beloved Cardinals or taking that prized once-a-year trip to St. Louis with his father to watch the Cardinals play baseball.

The boy wrote other things, too. Twice a month, he would drag out his father's old Underwood typewriter and slowly, one finger at a time, peck out on carbon-paper-thickened sheafs of paper the stories that made up his neighborhood "newspaper." Then he would stick one sheet behind the screen door of every house along his street. Once he even went to the neighborhood grocery store and asked, with great reluctance, if the grocer would buy an ad in the newspaper.

"How much would it cost?"

"Does a nickel sound like too much?"

"I think I can afford that. Go ahead and put in my ad—and here's a nickel."

It was a day the boy never forgot. His mother never forgot it either—not just that day but all of the days, when the boy sat and wrote in the tiny room with the shelves that were piled high with his collection of hundreds of Big-Little Books and Little-Big Books, each of which was numbered and catalogued on a master sheet that he had taped to the wall. The books cost a nickel apiece, and he bought a new one every Saturday . . . and read it by Monday.

Over the years the mother and father moved from house to house, but always the mother made it a point to find a safe place for the orange-and-black notebook. She never was sure why, except that the stories represented a piece of the boy, a piece that the passing of ever so many years never would diminish.

One day the boy, now a man, went to the attic of the old house to begin the tearful task of arranging for the auctioning of some of the furnishings. His mother had just died, six years after his father's death, and he felt so empty, alone, abandoned, like an orphan. He began to dig tenderly through boxes that housed the yesteryears of his life—a Lonnie Frey baseball glove, an autographed picture of Marty Marion, an electric football game, a 37-millimeter shell casing that an uncle had brought back from the war . . . and an orange-and-black notebook.

How is it possible that some people, myself among them, know from the very beginning what their life's work will be? I put that question to career consultant Gilles E. Richard, who said that I and those like me are the lucky people because, for the most part, we have been spared the occupational fires that have scorched so many. Why this happens to some people is not really understood, but Richard found at least two common denominators:

"As kids, they had a lot of nurturing from the parents, and, as a result, they always had a lot of self-confidence. Even when they were four or five, you could see that these kids were different . . . because they felt loved to an extraordinary degree. They were made to feel special."

"As these kids grew and did whatever it was, they were praised and rewarded—not only by their parents but also by their teachers, friends and peers. People recognized and supported their talents, and from a very early age they were surrounded by expressions of success. These things gave them affirmations that what they were doing was right for them."

I listened, and it occurred to me that Richard was saying essentially the same things that so many only children have told me about their lives—the accelerated achievement made possible by the nurturing, the feelings of being special, the praise and the rewards. This is a combination of factors that rarely comes together, except in only children, I suspect, but when it happens, it creates people "whose work is an expression of themselves," said Richard. In other words, for these people work isn't really work. It's almost like play, and it's as natural—and as necessary—as breathing, sleeping and eating.

I had to admit to Richard that I'd never thought about it quite that way, but I liked the sound of it. I was sure that Mom and Dad would like it, too, if they only knew. At that instant, I felt that somehow they did know, that the triangle still was intact.

In 1982, I finished my book *Father & Son: A Divorced Parent Discovers a Deeper Definition of Family,* which dealt with the reconciliation process after the parent-child bond has been emotionally splintered by divorce. Writing the book had a profound effect on me, like good therapy, because it enabled me to understand what had happened to me and my two sons after my divorce from their mother, why they had had the need to reject me, what was necessary to bring us back together. I never thought that writing anything else could ever touch me again so deeply, but I was wrong. In gathering my material and writing this book, I took many trips back in time, and I learned so much about myself and gained new insights into what it means to be an only child.

I better understand now why I sometimes take myself too seriously, why I don't always laugh when the joke's on me, why it's important for me to be recognized as special and to be treated that way, why I'm sometimes accused of acting like a retired Army colonel, why I attach myself so strongly to a few people and a few things and how losing them plays into my only-child fears of abandonment. I better understand now why I enjoy solitude, why I struggle during holidays when I'm thrown together with my wife's vast extended family, why I am fundamentally a solo act rather than a team player. I better understand my parents and their wounds and why they treated me as they did.

I think I appreciate myself more now, and like myself more, too, although the few people who knew me really well may wonder if that's possible. I think I'll be able to extend myself more to other people, to be more giving, accepting, understanding. I think I'm getting closer to being a more complete person, more open and less defended.

If there is one message I want to leave with only children who read this book, it is this: Only children need to understand how much they mean to their parents, how most of whatever happened in the growing-up process was built on what was intended to be pure love and healthy expectation. I think that only children, more than other children, can be healed by acceptance of parents as people who did the best they could with what they had to work with. We can ask no more of anybody, including ourselves.

A week before my father died unexpectedly of a heart attack, I had what would be my final conversation with him. I felt driven to tell him once more how important he was to me. "Dad, I'm so lucky to have you for my father." His response was immediate: "You can't know how good that makes me feel. I feel so good I just know they're going to have to shoot me on Judgment Day."

We all should feel so good, and it is my hope that someday we will.